PASSING THE TORCH

10/26/16

Don,

Your legacy in public
service is great! Thank you
for your continued work.
I hope you enjoy the book!

Charlotte Leweller Wilson

Follow your bliss!

Karl Besl

Passing the Torch

Planning for the Next Generation of Leaders in Public Service

KARL BESEL AND
CHARLOTTE LEWELLEN WILLIAMS

With Contributions from
Todd Bradley, Andreas Schmid, and Adam R. Smith

The University of Arkansas Press III Fayetteville III 2016

This book was made possible by the
University of Arkansas Clinton School of Public Service.

UNIVERSITY OF ARKANSAS
Clinton School of Public Service

CONTENTS

Foreword by James L. "Skip" Rutherford   vii

Introduction   ix

1 ¦¦¦ The State of Public Service in America   3
Karl Besel and Charlotte Lewellen Williams

2 ¦¦¦ Politics and Public Service   9
Todd Bradley and Karl Besel

3 ¦¦¦ Planning for the Next Generation
of Nonprofit Leaders   25
Karl Besel and Charlotte Lewellen Williams

4 ¦¦¦ International Differences in Nonprofit
Succession Planning   33
Karl Besel and Andreas Schmid

5 ¦¦¦ Succession Planning and Foundations   43
Charlotte Lewellen Williams and Karl Besel

6 ¦¦¦ Mergers, Acquisitions, and Leadership
in Health-Care Succession Planning   53
Adam R. Smith

References   67

Interviewees   73

Contributors   77

Index   79

FOREWORD

In *Passing the Torch*, professors Karl Besel and Charlotte Williams—through relying on their own expertise as well as tapping noted professionals—lay out a well-defined roadmap for the future of public service. Elevating the importance of organizational succession planning, Clinton School professor Williams and Clinton School visiting scholar Besel affirm an important Clinton School academic objective: leadership through civic engagement. Williams and Besel also highlight changing demographics and make a compelling case for public service organizations to do the same when planning for the future.

The Clinton School's Master of Public Service degree differs from more traditional graduate academic models in public administration, public affairs, and public policy because a significant portion of the school's curriculum is direct field service. This curriculum is also enriched with a speaker series, which the authors highlight. Williams and Besel understand, embrace and advocate the importance of developing new generations of leaders, which Dr. Sherece West, the CEO of the Winthrop Rockefeller Foundation, accurately calls "the bench."

Those who work in and with public-service, philanthropic, and health-care organizations; those who serve on related boards and commissions; and those in government and in the military should read this book, use it for reference and rely on it for future decision making. It should be required reading for those affiliated with AmeriCorps, Peace Corps, Teach for America, and other similar entities whose members and alumni will be assuming positions of public service leadership as millions of baby boomers like me leave the stage.

—James L. "Skip" Rutherford III,
dean University of Arkansas
Clinton School of Public Service

INTRODUCTION

During the fall semester of 2009, the Center on Community Philanthropy at the University of Arkansas Clinton School of Public Service appointed its inaugural Visiting Philanthropy Faculty Scholar. The Center on Community Philanthropy is part of the school dedicated to research, analysis, and learning about the concept of community-driven philanthropy as a way of delivering public service. The center's "Scholars in Residence" bring their collective knowledge to inform the field of public service and help build the evidence for community philanthropy as a powerful tool to promote social and economic equity. These scholars, who spend a semester at the Clinton School, are recruited from a diverse pool of academics, researchers, and practitioners from across the country. This particular year, our scholar, who spent his formative years in Southern California and professional life in the Midwest, Dr. Karl Besel, was somewhat apprehensive about this new adventure being embarked upon in the Deep South. Frankly, Little Rock, Arkansas, was far under the radar screen with regard to "must see and work there" places. To his surprise, he discovered a vibrant river city transformed over the last decade by a number of factors, including the strategic building of the Clinton Presidential Center, the Clinton Foundation, and the Clinton School of Public Service along the welcoming banks of the Arkansas River. This setting, which initially seemed both stately and subdued, became subject to periodic bursts of excitement as prominent officials, media personalities, and agency executives were weekly guests of the Clinton School Speaker Series or Scholar in Residence. These visitors during my (Karl Besel's) few months' stay in Little Rock ranged from CNN's John King and the W. K. Kellogg Foundation's Wenda Weeks-Moore to the ambassadors to Iraq and Afghanistan. President Clinton even made a lengthy appearance toward the end of my stay to serve as the keynote speaker for the School's five-year anniversary celebration, as well as the annual Christmas party.

All of these distinguished guests and scholars were generous with the time they devoted to the school's graduate students, and I enjoyed being along for the ride. One of my more memorable experiences was having dinner with Pulitzer Prize winner Taylor Branch, Dean Rutherford, and a couple Clinton School students. Shortly after the dinner started, Sacramento mayor and three-time NBA all-star Kevin Johnson joined us. The star-athlete-turned politician came with a stack of Branch's latest book (*The Clinton Tapes*) for the esteemed author to sign as Christmas presents. The dinner ended where it began, with the stack of books. Johnson politely asked for the books to be signed, and said "I wish I could write like you." Branch modestly lowered his head, smiled, and quipped "I remember watching you on TV . . . You can dunk. I can't [do] that!"

We tell this story to illustrate a key feature of the Clinton School experience. This series truly went beyond the confines of a forty-five-minute professional speech. Numerous opportunities were provided to student and faculty members alike to dialogue with weekly speakers. Through both formal and informal relationships with top leaders within a wide range of public-service fields, the Clinton School community was able to learn about the inspirations, motivations, and advisements, as well as the limitations of executives. The Washington D.C.-like experience with small-city Southern charm created by the deans, faculty, and staff at the Clinton School is one that cannot be easily replicated. Nonetheless, this project attempts to provide a variety of insights by gleaning information from a range of experts on a very timely subject. Like the Speaker Series, the chapter authors seek to foster an arena where informed dialogues can be commenced on how the next generation of public servants will be both recruited and motivated to lead organizations well in the twenty-first century. Important to this dialogue is the role that diversity will play in the next generation of nonprofit leadership, given the changing demographics of our country and the need to promote leadership that is ethnically, culturally, and racially diverse. To gather these insights, four questions were asked of each interviewee. The questions were:

1. What motivated you to embark upon a career within the public-service field?

2. What will motivate the next generation of executives (based upon the literature and interviews with executives) to become leaders within the public-service field?

3. What impact will negative views of public servants, as indicated through an increase in negative views of governmental officials, as well as grassroots anti-governmental movement (such as the Tea Party movement) have on recruiting public-service executives?

4. What are the main obstacles faced by current executives in succession planning and what role should diversity play in succession planning?

The chapters contained in this book aim to provide a variety of views and perspectives in the form of "profiles," or detailed interviews, with regard to one of the most pressing dilemmas faced by public and nonprofit organizations today. In tandem with the Clinton School Speaker Series, we invited a wide variety of accomplished professionals and officials to participate in discussions on executive succession planning with the authors, ranging from the current president and CEO of the largest healthcare nonprofit in the country, to people in their twenties who are already becoming elected officials. We use their stories and insights in order to place data on executive retirements within a rich and broad context.

The profiles we use as a vehicle for discussing the state of public service in America, as well as its most compelling leadership challenges, are intended to capture the intellectual richness of a highly respected speaker series. Much like the Clinton School Speaker Series, we feature a wide variety of viewpoints from public-service experts.

Chapter 1 focuses on the state of public service in America, including what distinguishes this sector in our country from those civil-society institutions in other nations. Chapter 2 in many ways serves as a bridge between chapter 1 and subsequent chapters by expanding upon the nature of public service in the United States, especially as this topic pertains to elected officials, as well as beginning a dialogue about some of the challenges faced by the sector.

Chapters 3 through 6 highlight the leadership challenges faced by this sector, especially with regard to executive-level succession planning. While the for-profit sector has been fostering strategies for intentional succession planning for decades, both the public and nonprofit sectors have lagged behind their proprietary counterparts in this area. The executives interviewed for these chapters ranged from nonprofit training and networking institutions (the Independent Sector) to leaders of a number of health-care organizations. Most of these interviewees lead health-care organizations because this sector will continue to surpass all other industries in job growth over the next decade. Between 2012 and 2022, the number of jobs in health services management will increase by twenty-three percent. In contrast to this dramatic jump in occupational opportunities in health-care management, the total projected increase for all occupations is eleven percent, while non-health-care management positions are only anticipated to increase by seven percent during the same time period (Bureau of Labor Statistics 2015). Thus, if a remake of the 1967 Academy Award winning movie The Graduate were made today, the advice provided to the young college graduate (played by Dustin Hoffman) that "there's a great future in plastics" would probably be updated to "there's a great future in health-care management." That being said, the plastics industry continues to be extremely viable!

Through the collection of interviews presented in the following chapters, we seek to provide an open door to a number of "corner offices" occupied by some of the most accomplished and prominent public-service executives. We hope that our readers will benefit from the candid and occasionally unconventional perspectives provided by experts who have already proven themselves within this precarious and often misunderstood field. This book does not seek to provide comprehensive analysis on the public-service sector, but rather to highlight key components of this field, as well as provide insights related to intentional succession planning.

Ultimately our goal is to broaden the scope of infrastructure development for the public-service sector. Through this project we aim to illuminate areas of contrast between existing public-service leaders, identify themes of motivation for their service, and develop a pathway for cultivating the next generation of diverse, talented, and committed leaders in public service.

PASSING THE TORCH

1 ||| The State of Public Service in America

KARL BESEL AND
CHARLOTTE LEWELLEN WILLIAMS

What Makes the American Public Service Field Distinct: A Historical and Prospective Review

Philosopher Alexis de Tocqueville was probably the first individual to document the distinctiveness of public service in the United States. While Tocqueville's travels throughout this emerging nation took place when the American republic was only around four decades old, he observed that a surprising number of voluntary associations had already developed. Tocqueville commented as much, if not more so, on the American spirit of voluntarism and associational life as he did on American individualism.

As a native Frenchman, Tocqueville was struck by this pattern of American cooperation. Much like the United States, his country had also experienced a violent revolution to squash a monarch's absolute control over its citizenry. As detailed by Wilson (1989), the French aimed to place checks on the authority of their leaders following their revolution in the only way they knew how—through laws and rules imposed upon elected officials, as well as upon bureaucrats. Thus, centralized governmental authority was not eliminated by the French Revolution— it was compelled to become more responsive to the citizenry through the initiation of popular elections and more equitable laws and rules. This legacy of legalism and formalism has shaped French conduct to the present.

While the American revolutionists embraced many of the same ideals as the French revolutionists, the former English colonists decided to follow a different path with regard to how power would be distributed in governing structures. There was scarcely a central government before or long after the revolution. Subsequently, the survival of citizens within this largely agrarian nation was dependent not on the benevolence of an aristocrat, but typically on the level of cooperation exhibited by neighboring farmers. Cooperation was encouraged by a desire to subdue the wilderness, as well as by the self-governing principles of Protestant churches. This tradition of political and religious self-government was so strong that it nearly prevented the ratification of the Constitution, which in turn fostered the creation of a government with limited powers, especially in comparison to its European counterparts.

The modern-day public-service sector in the United States that sprouted from the nineteenth-century compromise between individualism and collective responsibility has evolved into a system of third-party government and a patchy welfare state (Salamon 1999). The American nonprofit sector, which remained relatively small throughout most of twentieth century, began to grow at an accelerated rate in the 1970s. The nonprofit sector produced 4.2 percent of gross domestic product in 2000—up from 3.1 percent in 1970. By contrast, the government sector produced 10.8 percent of the GDP in 2000 (down from 13.9 percent in 1970), while the business sector produced 84.9 percent of all goods and services during this same time period (Bureau of Economic Analysis 2001). At face value it appears that these changes in revenue indicate a decline in influence by the government sector in tandem with an expansion of the nonprofit sector. As articulated by Powell and Steinberg (2006), one must look behind these numbers in order to accurately assess the changing fiscal dynamics over the past few decades. From 1970 to 2000, the government sector's participation in the direct production of output, primarily in the defense budget, certainly did decline. Nonetheless, during this same time period, governmental expenditures increased with regard to making transfers for others to spend, as in social security payments or contracting out for services. Thus, the continuing growth of the nonprofit sector into the twenty-first century (gross domestic product increased to 5.5 percent in 2010) must acknowledge the interdependence between these sectors (Bureau of Economic Analysis 2013). Salamon's (1999) previously mentioned description of the American nonprofit-management field as evolving into a "third sector government and patchy welfare state" poignantly articulates why teasing out nonprofit revenue increases from governmental ones is a difficult, if not impossible, task. The symbiotic relationship that has developed between nonprofit and public entities over the past two centuries makes it problematic to discern where one sector ends and the other one begins.

A Case for Executive Succession Planning

Succession planning has been described as a systematic and long-term practice that an organization follows to ensure it has the necessary pool of managerial talent to enable it to meet its business objectives and achieve its mission (Rothwell 2002). The prevailing view in the literature is that a formalized process of succession planning should be followed. The considerable expansion of the nonprofit sector over the last few decades, along with the anticipated number of executives who will reach retirement age over the next two decades, also seems to warrant the implementation of this process. Public-service executives, both elected and appointed, within the public and nonprofit sectors, will be retiring at record levels within the next two decades. More than 2.8 million executives reached the age of sixty-five in 2011; annual numbers of executives reaching age sixty-five will consistently rise for the next ten years, surpassing four million by 2020 (Census Bureau, Population Division 2012). Finding qualified, motivated leaders to fill all the vital executive positions vacated by this generation is going to present pressing challenges within both the public and nonprofit sectors.

This mounting crisis in executive leadership within the public-service sector demands immediate attention in light of the pivotal role played by organizational leaders. This central role played by executive leaders with regard to organizational viability within both governmental and nonprofit organizations has been recognized for many decades. An early empirical study found that charismatic leaders, with professional independence and idealism, have potent influence on the direction and performance of nonprofit organizations (Newman and Wallender 1978). Within the public sector, Wilson (1989) points to the central role played by executives in fostering greater levels of innovation needed to perpetuate organizational viability. Later work by Herman and Heimovics (1989, 1990, 1994) reinforces the notion of the chief executive as the single most critical factor underlying nonprofit effectiveness. They conclude that "chief executives occupy a place of psychological centrality" and "are assigned and accept responsibility for both successful and unsuccessful outcomes," whereas "board presidents see themselves as affecting outcomes little" (Herman and Heimovics 1990, 171).

Despite the considerable growth in the nonprofit sector, and central role of executives in leading these organizations, Froelich, McKee, and Rathge (2011) found in their survey analysis of eight hundred charitable organizations [tax exempt under Internal Revenue Code 501(c)(3)] and 859 cooperatives [IRS Code 501(c)(4)] that while nonprofit board members and hired executives deem succession planning to be important, few have implemented strategic plans for replacing their key leaders. This study concluded that nonprofits often exhibit a notable disconnect between the perceived importance of succession planning and actual concrete actions undertaken toward succession planning The paltry board preparation for succession seems indicative of a rose-colored glasses approach, possibly stemming from the paradox of a long-serving leader imparting a mind-set of stability (15).

The Changing Landscape of America

The case for succession planning in the nonprofit sector must also be analyzed through the lens of an increasingly changing racial and ethnic makeup of America. It is anticipated that the United States will experience a demographic shift between 2000 and 2050, making it a minority majority country with the biggest shift resulting from the growth in the population of immigrants and their children. Even though the number of African Americans in the United States has remained unchanged between 1970 and today, and projections indicate this will remain so, the numbers of Asians and Latinos have been increasing dramatically. Not only have numbers of immigrant populations been rising, they have also begun locating to different urban settings and states around the country. (Lewellwn Williams, Rutherford, and Hoffpauir 2013). For example, data shows that instead of settling into the central city and later migrating to suburbs as economic growth occurs, a phenomena known as "spatial assimilation" Lewellen Williams, Rutherford, and Hoffpauir (2013) show many immigrants are choosing to land directly in suburbs. Another evolving location dynamic is immigrants moving to states other than traditional choices (Singer 2004; Zuniga and Hernandez-Leon 2006) and one of the target new locations is the South, especially what is referred to as the Deep South. This increase in number and range of new residents will require not only an open-minded approach to welcoming these individuals and families, but also a parallel commitment to fostering programs and services designed to accelerate their integration into the social and economic fabric of America. An important component of this integration work will likely take place at the state and local level, where nonprofit organizations have first point of contact with these newcomers, whether through getting driver's licenses, enrolling their kids in schools, or learning English. The nonprofit sector will undoubtedly play a major role in creating the safety nets within communities to help ensure economic mobility for, civic participation by, and societal openness to immigrants. (Lewellen Williams, Rutherford, and Hoffpauir 2013).

Consequently, leadership within the nonprofit sector should begin to be more reflective of the populations they serve, meaning more diversity in president, CEO and director-level positions within nonprofit organizations must begin to emerge if in fact they intend to be representative of and attuned to the need for inclusion within the sector. This includes the ongoing call for more African American, Asian, and Latino leaders in nonprofit organizations, which sets the stage for black and immigrant communities to organize around preparing and lifting up a generation of nonprofit leaders.

So the question of succession planning begins to take on an even more complex nature in light of the changing demographics of America. How succession planning should respond to changing populations is a question for consideration. However, the lack of emphasis placed on succession planning and the measly board preparation in succession planning seems to indicate that this is an area greatly in need of new thinking.

2 ||| Politics and Public Service

TODD BRADLEY AND KARL BESEL

President John F. Kennedy's famous "ask not what your country can do for you, ask what you can do for your country" speech inspired many young people in the 1960s to dedicate themselves to public service.

A key question this chapter attempts to answer is what will motivate members of generation Y to embark upon careers in public service in a politically polarized, Tea Party world?

Description of Study

In order to gain insight with regard to this question we interviewed a number of elected officials, ranging from one of the youngest mayors in the country (Chris McBarnes) to one of the most distinguished and longest-serving national congressional representatives (retired U.S. Rep. Lee Hamilton). We intentionally selected a generationally diverse group of officials in order to assess different perceptions between age cohorts, as well as commonalities. Motivating Crowding Theory is employed as a theoretical framework for guiding this discussion. The impact of anti-governmental groups such as the Tea Party on public service motivation, especially on members of generation Y, is also explored.

Motivating Crowding Theory

Motivating Crowd Theory grew out of the disciplines of economics, psychology, and later, sociology. The basic premise is that there are two ways people are motivated. There is extrinsic motivation (economics), or, incentives coming from outside the person; and there is intrinsic motivation (psychology), that is, motives that come from within the person (Frey and Jegen 2001). The theory stipulates a systematic interaction between extrinsic and intrinsic motivation. More recent research on motivation in the public sector, labeled other-oriented motives, focuses on reciprocity styles: taking, giving, and matching (Grant 2013). Grant suggests that there are three primary styles of motivation in the public sector (although such styles can exist in the private sector as well). Takers are persons who strategically help others if they will receive more than they give. Givers are people who operate on an opposite principle: they are willing to give first when the benefits to others outweigh the personal costs. Matchers fall in the middle of the reciprocity spectrum: they try to preserve an even balance of giving and receiving, they believe in quid pro quo ("you scratch my back, and I'll scratch yours"). But, as Mark Twain quipped, "the principle of give and take is the principle of diplomacy—give one and take ten." Fortunately, Twain's quote is hyperbole (some would say only slightly exaggerated). Past and current research illustrates there is a myriad of factors that motivate people to engage in public-sector work.

There are ongoing challenges faced by the public sector, but perhaps even more so at the local government level, because of the growing disdain for "big" government. Although, we must note, "big" government is in the eyes of the beholder, because when one's needs are being met and services are being fulfilled, whether as an individual voter or corporation, the notion of "big" government becomes unimportant. Nevertheless, the evolving roles and responsibilities of local governments are fueling the gap between government legitimacy and administrative responsibility. As Nalbandian, et al. (2013, 571) point out, especially when it comes to leadership in local government leaders must:

> Integrate citizen and other forms of engagement [planned and spontaneous, including social media] with traditional local government structures and processes.

Collaborative engagement, the focus of the third leadership challenge [retaining future leaders in light of private-sector opportunities for those leaders], is a mechanism that can be employed to coordinate disparate structures of authority, turning them into working networks. While this leadership challenge complements the second challenge, it should not be confused with it; the second challenge focuses on the importance of structure when working within a networked environment, while the third challenge's focus is collaborative engagement as a process.

We will discuss, in our concluding remarks, some implications of Motivating Crowd Theory in the context of our interviews.

Interviewees

The following public sector executives were interviewed:

> former United States Rep. Lee Hamilton (D-IN)
>
> former two-term San Francisco mayor Willie Brown
>
> former NBA all-star and current Sacramento mayor Kevin Johnson
>
> Columbus, Ohio, mayor Michael Coleman
>
> Mayor Chris McBarnes of Frankfort, Indiana
>
> Lloyd Dean, CEO of Dignity Health

All interviews were conducted between March and October 2013, either in person or via telephone. In addition to representing a range of generations (World War II through generation Y), efforts were made to recruit both former and current public officials from geographically and politically diverse regions of the country.

Intrinsic Motivating Factors of the Interviewees

As one might expect, intrinsic catalysts for embarking on a career in public service ended up being consistent with all the officials interviewed. Nonetheless, the officials interviewed varied in the way they articulated what sparked their enthusiasm for careers in public service. Both McBarnes and Hamilton, officials on each end of the generational spectrum, spoke in more abstract terms about motivational sources. Hamilton stated that he "wanted to contribute to the success of representative democracy" (Hamilton, pers. comm.). McBarnes said he was "legacy-driven" and that he "did not want to be remembered as a politician, but wanted to be remembered as a leader in public policy" (McBarnes, pers. comm.).

Dean said having "very little access to healthcare growing up" motivated him "to embark upon a career in the public service field" (Dean, pers. comm.). He said that his parents always emphasized the importance of education. Dean said he was a teacher for a while after college, but eventually was recruited by Upjohn Pharmaceutical Company. He "always wanted to give back, because he had so little growing up."

In contrast with speaking in a more general sense about being driven by desire to improve their communities and country, mayors Brown, Johnson, and Coleman discussed their personal journeys that led them to careers in elected office. Brown captured how volunteer activities and friendships he made as a college student continue to motivate his commitment to public service:

> In the early 1950s, when entering San Francisco State University, it was clearly an activist political campus, and I met a guy on the first day who I became life-long friends [with], and who is currently the chair of the Democratic State [California] Central Committee, and, secondly, I was recruited by the Alpha Phi Alpha Fraternity and recruited by the NAACP Youth Chapter, and the church that I attended was made up of the political elite of the African American community of San Francisco, and having being raised in Mineola, Texas, and living the trials and tribulations of an African American, I realized that I was not being given an equal chance, thus all of these experiences provided a platform for me to be agitating for solutions to problems, which was the foundation for why I got started in public service. (Brown, pers. comm.)

Coleman and Johnson also elaborated about the lasting impact of early influences on their career decisions. Coleman's encounter with Supreme Court Justice Thurgood Marshall as an intern greatly impacted his decision to pursue public service as a career, he said:

> From a young age, I was always motivated by a desire to change the world. One particularly inspiring incident took place when I was fortunate enough to be interning with the Carter White House and had the opportunity to meet Thurgood Marshall. I told him I was going to be a lawyer, and he said, "OK. What are you going to do with that?" It reminded me that whatever career success I had was only as good as the lives I could touch with it. (Coleman, pers. comm.)

As a three-time NBA all-star and graduate of one the nation's most prestigious universities, Johnson possessed a wide range of job options following his successful career as a professional athlete. The following story about his grandfather continues to influence his philosophy on the importance of public service:

> My grandfather was a sheet metal worker . . . a hard worker, he had routine and structure. He believed in working hard and treating people fair, and giving back to the community. It wasn't a complicated philosophy—a man with simple values. You know Martin Luther King has the famous quote that "times of challenge and controversy are really when we have to give back and make a difference." It's the test of our character. Not just what's convenient and comfortable. I think my grandfather epitomizes what a neighbor was about. If any opportunity presented itself, such as someone running out of gas, he would pull out his gas tank and help out. If someone had a flat tire, he would do the same thing. And it was basically being a good neighbor when the opportunity presented itself, not just when it was convenient. That's something that was instilled in me . . . to always vote and give back, and make a difference in your community—no matter how big or small. And I think those early influences are what led me to run for mayor

because public service is the highest way and highest form of really giving back. I'm very thankful. (Johnson, pers. comm.)

The officials interviewed considered their time spent as public servants as a privilege not to be taken for granted. On the other hand, motivations were not always novel or inspirational. In addition to being influenced by a desire to "continue to the success of representative democracy," as previous mentioned, Hamilton also stated he was "bored with practicing law and being an attorney" (Hamilton, pers. comm.). To him, being a politician just seemed like a more interesting way of making a living.

Impact of Negative Views of Public Service

Public executive leaders must be adept at not only maneuvering the labyrinth of local, state, and federal bureaucratic legislation, but they must also appease the often whimsical and unpredictable citizenry. Or as Hahm, Jung, and Moon (2013, 178) suggested, "an effective public corporation leader must be a skillful politician and businessperson, as public corporations often operate in an environment in which public and private values interact."

Historically, there have been many groups (including the current Tea Party in American politics), which have thrust their distrust toward any entity even faintly representing the government. The Tea Party can be seen as a type of trigger, or "origin of conflict" (Chappell 2007). Origins of conflict can be employee instigated and/or initiated by outside forces. Such groups have been suspicious of public-sector notions more broadly, including public-sector goods and services such as Medicare/Medicaid and other forms of healthcare. "For public administrators, it is important to understand [the conflict's] sources, evaluate its impacts, adjust to its pressures, and make decisions consistent with current goals and issues while staying within the political and statutory limits of their jurisdiction. Conflict administration is an important step in that direction" (Chappell 2007, 39). Thus, the challenges that face public-sector executives have been made more difficult, beyond the generic notion of "the public." We might call challenges "wicked problems" as Rittel and Webber (1973) named them. Such "wicked problems" might be today's contentious health-care debates. Nevertheless, public-sector executives are up for the challenges.

When asked "What impact will negative views of public servants, as indicated through an increase in negative views of governmental officials, as well as grassroots anti-governmental movements (such as the Tea Party) have on recruiting public-service executives?" Hamilton said, "I don't worry much about it, because the U.S. has such a talented pool in both private and public sectors." He went on to say that "the real problem is high turnover in the public sector" and that "recruiting such talent is not the problem, but retention is the problem" (Hamilton, pers. comm.).

Coleman said there "will always be those who promote a negative view of public service. But I don't believe those individuals will have any significant effect on the number of people who want to serve their communities. The call to service in this country is far too powerful to be dampened by a reactive political movement" (Coleman, pers. comm.).

Dean noted "the current environment has not been helpful to the public sector in general (including the ultimate public executive, President Obama). The need for coalitions is of the utmost importance."

Dean said building professional relationships across various fields will help minimize blowback from groups such as the Tea Party. The coalitions will reveal that the majority of Americans believe in creating fair and adequate access to the many opportunities that should be available in our country. Dean went on to suggest that motivating the next generation of public-service executives will mean, "being a good example, that you can make a difference, as well as emphasizing lots of health-care opportunities" (Dean, pers. comm.)

Brown suggested because of the demands and constant assumptions, like not meeting certain ethical standards, it is "unattractive for people that want to do public life, and the advent of technology like social media and the unbridled and uncontrolled use of the social media which represent (and in some cases misrepresent) what people really stand for, usually is a downer for people that want to go into public office, because they just don't care to be examined excruciatingly as is the case today, which makes the negatives much higher from that perspective, compared to when I came along. It was perceived as instantly an honor to be in the public world (when I entered public life years ago), in fact [now] we are seeing just the opposite, and that is dissuading people from wanting to serve" (Brown, pers. comm.).

On the other hand, concern about groups such as the Tea Party and their ambivalence to public-sector work was viewed differently by McBarnes. He said such groups as the Tea Party have valid concerns, especially when it comes to the perception (and at times reality) that there is rampant government waste. McBarnes' mission has four cornerstones, including citizen voice, which does not exclude any voices, including the Tea Party, at least in Frankfort, Indiana. The other three cornerstones —neighborhood revitalization, economic development, and communications—are essential for a public-policy leader to focus on, especially at the local level. McBarnes said he believes in private/public partnerships and the pooling of resources to help nurture economic development in Frankfort (McBarnes, pers. comm.). As O'Toole (1997) pointed out, fostering networks (what we might call partnerships in the twenty-first century), with organizations is a key component of public-service leadership.

"Networks are structures of interdependence involving multiple organizations of parts thereof," he wrote. More recently, researchers such as Waring, Currie, and Bishop (2013) have illustrated how public-private partnerships vary and advised that service innovations should include notions of "upstream" (strategic orientation) and "downstream" (organization of work) outcomes in their decision-making. Thus, whether the collaborations are in local government or nonprofits, establishing linkages helps maintain the public's perception of the organization's legitimacy, and the need for public goods and services.

Motivating Generation Y

Public-service motivation and job performance are essential linkages to continual delivery of public goods and services (Belle 2013). Belle's primary findings suggested that an employee who had direct contact with beneficiaries of public goods and services was more likely to have higher job satisfaction. Public-service motivation is a fluid process. "Both contact with program beneficiaries and self-persuasion interventions induced larger increases in performance among employees self-reporting stronger PSM before being exposed to these two experimental conditions," Belle reported (150). However, will such motivation and performance "standards" hold up in non-hospital settings (Belle's study was in a hospital), where one-on-contact is the daily norm, compared to public services, which may not always be as intimate?

What will motivate the next generation of public-service executives to become leaders within the public-service field? Hamilton said:

> motivating the next generation may include issues of worker satisfaction (however there is an impressive number of young people available). The younger generation may be more interested in making more money (but there are areas in the public sector that are just as competitive as the private sector, e.g., federal judges), in the private sector (which complicates retention). However, there are many young people that are interested in more than simply making more money, but are looking for more challenges, especially in a large, diverse democracy like the United States. Moreover, the younger generation may be seeking the sheer challenges of public-sector work; and interested in the common good, as opposed to the individualism of the market-based, private sector. (Hamilton, pers. comm.)

"I am of the opinion that there will not be the kinds of enrichment opportunities for the next generation, because the training process that preceded my generation and affected my generation is not continuously available to the next generation because there is not the same clear and dramatic definition of need," Brown said. "The new leadership will come from dedication, the individual motivation and the public demand, rather than from the motivation gained from associations and in membership organizations and personal experiences" (Brown, pers. comm.).

In contrast to Brown's view, Johnson perceived public service as potentially more viable with members of generation Y as a result of social media and more of a commitment to "doing something about the environment and climate change." Johnson said he didn't want to "sell any generation short," because a desire to engage in public service goes back to "Ben Franklin and the volunteer fire department." Johnson also emphasized that "all of our national leaders have made public service a top priority" and these activities are an ingrained part of American culture and society (Johnson, pers. comm.).

On a final note to this discussion, generation Y mayor McBarnes stated that Robert Greenleaf (1904–90), the founder of the modern servant leadership movement, and his notion of "the servant as leader," motivated him to get involved in politics at an early age (McBarnes, pers. comm.). McBarnes became one of the youngest mayors in the country (and the youngest in the state of Indiana), at age twenty-three.

There is no "silver bullet" to motivate current and potential employees; what will work varies across time and space. There are many pieces to the puzzle. That is, "recruiting and hiring employees with strong public-service values will only work if the recruits perceive that their tasks are important and that they work in environments that enable them to act on their motivations" (Paarlberg and Lavigna 2010, 716).

Main Obstacles Faced by Public-Sector Executives

There is a myriad of obstacles (or what some might call opportunities) that public-service executives face, including tight budgets and perceptions. Perry and Buckwalter's (2010) research looks back to Leonard White's *The Future of Government in the United States: Essays in Honor of Charles E. Merriam* (1942), as they envision what public service might look like in 2020. Their vision includes White's twentieth-century challenges, which are "global or national, economic, political or managerial, racial, community, ideological" (White 1942, 192). Ideological challenges include movements like the Tea Party, contentious legislation such as "stand your ground" laws, what some might call self-defense, and Second amendment issues.

Perry and Buckwalter suggest three broad developments to improved standing of public service as we approach 2020: new political realities and rhetoric, generational transformations, and normal reassent of public service. The contributions of public service will yield greater acceptance of the centrality of government to national survival and achievement," they say, noting that "to some extent, growth in acceptance is event driven" (240). For example, they point to the 1995 bombing of the Murrah Federal Building in Oklahoma City, and the terrorist attacks of September 11, 2001, as examples of events that reasserted acceptance of public-sector leadership. Furthermore, the election of Barack Obama as president harkened back to White's assumptions regarding racial and ideological lines as being potential challenges to public-service leadership.

Generational transformations, "shifting patterns of public-regardingness across generations," are reflected in recent trends (241), such as the Higher Education Research Institute's data, which illustrates an upward trend (since 1997) in college freshman volunteerism. Normal reassent of public service requires reinvigorating public-sector work, which includes competitive wages/salaries and retirement packages compared to the private sector. Lastly, "the replacement of the Baby Boom generation will, by itself, create public service demand and opportunities that have not existed since the 1970s," Perry and Buckwalter write. The changes are less the result of growth as they are the exit of masses of job incumbents moving to another stage of their lives" (244). In general, people are oriented to act in the public sector for the purpose of doing good in the public sphere. Motivation is driven by other behavior, not just self-concern and self-interest. Public-service motivation varies around the world; in some countries the meaning of public-service motivation is less institutionalized (Perry, Hondeghem, and Wise 2010).

Public-sector executives must have various types of capital at their disposal: political leadership capital, managerial leadership capital, and individual leadership capital (Hahm, Jung, and Moon 2012). Political leadership capital involves securing political support (for example, support from Congress) for new initiatives and defending organizational interests by coping with unfavorable political influence such as Tea Party blowback. Managerial leadership capital includes providing new visions and strategies and securing organizational members' support for internal organizational, personnel, and financial management. Public-sector leadership involves individual leadership capital, that is, public-sector executives should have professional credentials and traits such as professional experience, commitment, and trust of their employees.

Hahm, Jung, and Moon (2012) lucidly demonstrate that leadership capital in its various forms is essential for sustaining a successful, vigorous organization, whether the organization is a billion-dollar nonprofit firm like Kaiser Permanente or Congress. Such skills are required to meet the multiple obstacles faced by public-sector executives, whether those challenges are internal, external, or both. Dean said Dignity Health, for example, is focused on diversity, training programs (including cultural sensitivity at all levels), forming coalitions with colleges and universities (similar to the mentoring program with Spelman College), and setting examples at Dignity Health, including in his own capacity as chief executive officer. "We are fortunate in the United States to have people of color and diversity and able to access knowledge and seize the opportunity," Dean said (Dean, pers. comm.). Hamilton noted "public sector leadership planning is not easy" especially when you are competing in financial terms with the private sector. Also, budget battles, especially on Capitol Hill, where he represented the Ninth Congressional District of Indiana for thirty-four years, and creating incentives for staff are ongoing challenges. He went onto say "in the case of federal judges, you typically don't have succession planning issues" because the salaries are competitive compared to the private sector and judges are appointed for life.

"In the executive branch [presidential cabinet-level], there is less flexibility with regard to leadership succession planning," he said, adding that retention is always an issue, as well as incentives and that a pool of quality leaders is always important (Hamilton, pers. comm.).

Brown explained how his institute helps to build skills that are essential to navigating a life in public service.

"At the Willie Brown Institute, I've attempted to attract, guide, and train people into public life, either from the appointment or electoral standpoint, I believe that [through] the appointment process, if one can weather that storm or perform the tasks, one can gain the skills for them to survive the onslaught of the bloggers, investigatory reporters and others that are constantly looking for the opportunity to embarrass," he said. "If the Willie Brown Institute can equip people to be better prepared, better informed, and more scrupulous about their personal conduct then they will be able to handle the negatives and they will be OK." He ended our conversation by saying "the highest calling in this world that anyone can gain is the opportunity to be elected to public office, I really do believe that is ultimately more rewarding emotionally, intellectually, and the talent that you have, you share with your fellow people in this democracy, no matter what the pitfalls are, in terms of exposure" (Brown, pers. comm.)

Implications and Why Motivating Crowd Theory Matters in Public-Sector Executive Leadership

Public-sector executive leadership motivation relates to the notion that individuals are attracted to work and leadership positioning in the public sector because it provides them the opportunity of doing good for others and for society. Beyond traditional notions of the extrinsic value of social standing in the community attached to being a public servant are the intrinsic reasons. Against the backdrop of public scrutiny, public-sector executive leaders face continuing budgetary concerns and increasing calls for efficiency, as well as criticism of effectiveness in the delivery of services. Budgetary concerns may result in even more limited access to health care, as Dean experienced while growing up. As well, it is critical that public-sector executives are keenly aware of the salience of fostering and supporting the intrinsic motivations of employees. A great example of having an intentional mission of keeping employees (and potential employees) intrinsically motivated is demonstrated by the linkage of Dignity Health with Spelman College. The "pipeline" of developing future public-sector executives is being nurtured at Spelman College (an all-women's historically black college), which also enhances diversity efforts, an important part of Dignity Health's mission.

Throughout our interviews, the interviewees demonstrated another commitment to intrinsic values. The leaders saw it necessary to model behaviors that extend beyond private-sector notions of simply making money. They said leading by example in exhibiting values that transcend self-interest, and proving themselves to be trustworthy, are much more enduring motivators than simply financial gain.

As Hamilton noted earlier, it can be difficult for public-sector jobs to compete in terms of income with private-sector opportunities, but there are other ways of motivating public-sector executives in terms of how the employees can contribute. It is important that public-sector leaders continue to develop and support best practices, appropriate to a public-sector environment. For example, value-based leadership (placing the common good over individual gains), a supportive work environment, organizational goals, and job characteristics that reflect employees' public-sector intrinsic motivation have been shown to have a positive impact on morale and performance. The notion of value-based leadership is summed up well in Johnson's sentiments: "all of our national leaders have made public service a top priority" (Johnson, pers. comm.). These activities are an ingrained part of American culture and society, which mirror the consequences of Motivating Crowd Theory, which should enable public-sector leaders to continue to nurture the next generation of public-sector servants.

Patterns of Discernment

What patterns can we discern from the various public officials in terms of why people get involved in public-sector employment, motivating the next generation of public-sector leaders, challenges and so on? A sense of civic duty seems to be apparent in why people engage in public-sector occupations. Often this desire to make a contribution to one's community is fostered by close friends and family members early in life. Consequently, public-sector executives want to make a positive difference in people's lives, individually and collectively. Public-service executives want to give back to communities as a whole, and feel in many ways a calling to have a positive impact on people's lives. On the other hand, being an elected official may appear to be a more intriguing career path than what is offered by the private sector. As noted by Grant (2013), motivations to engage in public-service careers are often complex, and cannot be classified as merely intrinsic or external.

Overall, the elected officials interviewed were optimistic about being able to motivate members of generation Y to engage in public service. Their commitment to issues ranging from the environment to social justice was perceived to be stronger than the potential threat posed by antigovernmental groups. The potential negative impact of groups such as the Tea Party was viewed as short-lived at best, especially in light of the average age of members of this grassroots movement.

Recommendations and Challenges

Public-sector leaders will always have to contend with the political environment. They will also need to reflect on what is unique about public-sector careers and the importance of a public-sector philosophy that undoubtedly places obligations and responsibilities on public servants beyond those required of private-sector employees. In terms of competing with private-sector salaries, public-sector dollars may be generally lower, but if they are at least somewhat consistent with private sector pay, the intrinsic motivation may still prevail. Additionally, public-sector leaders will continually need to minimize growing antigovernment emotions from movements like the Tea Party and articulate the virtues of serving the common good. As well, it is salient to remember that "any changes in the terms and conditions, in the very broadest sense, under which public servants work, impacts on the image and identity of public servants and raises the question of whether this new image will motivate people to enter public service" (O'Riordan 2013, 31).

3 ▌▌▌ Planning for the Next Generation of Nonprofit Leaders

KARL BESEL AND CHARLOTTE LEWELLEN WILLIAMS

When I (Karl Besel) accepted my first executive-level position as a director of a small, court-related nonprofit, the transition from my predecessor's tenure as director to my start as the new CEO was anything but planned. My predecessor was fired, and I subsequently took over as the agency's new leader with a board with divided loyalties. Some members were friends with my predecessor; others played instrumental roles in her removal from the position. After five years passed and I announced my decision to leave the agency, not much had changed with regard to executive succession planning. I was initially placed in charge of finding my replacement, which ended up being awkward at best. When I was eventually able to delegate this responsibility to the board president and a few other board members, I quickly became apprehensive about their ability to screen applicants for the job fairly. For example, when an applicant's file from the Urban League was being reviewed, the consensus on his application was that "he probably wouldn't be a good fit for this community." The agency served a predominately white, suburban locality outside of Indianapolis, and this quote epitomizes the insular mindset held by many longstanding members of this particular community.

I share this story to illustrate a number of points about executive succession planning with nonprofits. First off, while most organizations are increasingly acknowledging the critical role of succession planning prior to an executive's departure, few have plans in place to guide them through the process (Gothard and Austin 2013; Austin and Salkowitz 2009; Bell, Moyers, and Wolfred 2006). Secondly, a disconnect exists between the prevailing literature and actual organizational practices with regard to appropriate roles in succession planning. The consensus with organizational research studies is that leadership succession planning is ultimately the board's responsibility, yet boards often rely on their executive directors to initiate the planning processes (Bell, Moyers, and Wolfred 2006; Dalton and Dalton 2007). Lastly, diversity remains a pervasive issue that needs to be proactively addressed by board members. In their survey analysis of almost two thousand nonprofit executives in eight cities, Bell, Moyers, and Wolfred (2006) found that nonprofit executives were overwhelmingly white (eight-two percent). Subsequently, Halpern (2006) found that while women made up the majority of agency leaders, fifty-five percent of organizations with budgets of more than five million dollars a year were operated by male executives.

Description of Study

This chapter consists of interviews with CEOs of nonprofits who were able to work in tandem with their boards to shift from traditional replacement-succession planning toward a more comprehensive succession-management approach. Succession management is defined as "formal, ongoing, holistic, and strategic management that builds a reliable supply of talent throughout the organization" (Froelich, McKee, and Rathge, 2011). Succession management also includes the search for talent from both internal and external managerial pools, linking selection criteria to a candidate's specific competencies. Essentially, these interviews provide insight with regard to how organizations can foster a "culture of succession management" where nonprofit administrators partner with board members in the development of leaders whose strengths and experiences fit the organization's mission and values (Cao, Maruping, and Takeuchi, 2006). Interviews were conducted with Diana Aviv, president and CEO of the Independent Sector; Pierre Ferrari, CEO of Heifer Inc.; and Barnard Tyson, chairman and CEO of Kaiser Permanente. The additional benefit of incorporating an interview with Aviv was the ability to glean information about how smaller nonprofits could adapt succession-management models used by larger nonprofits. Aviv's organization, the largest networking organization for nonprofits in the United States, regularly disseminates information and provides training throughout the country on organizational leadership. These interviews took place between January and October 2013.

Board Involvement in Succession Management

A consistent theme throughout the interviews was the fundamental role played by the boards of directors in leadership development. Tyson stated that "Annually we spend a whole day with the board where we [organizational administrators] have to bring forward our succession plan and top candidates for key roles across the company" (Tyson, pers. comm.)

In the case of Heifer, Ferrari pointed out that "while the board did not conduct succession planning" before he became the CEO, "a specific mandate now exists" for the board to be involved in managing this process. A primary component of succession management at Heifer consists of "having each of our executives identify three potential successors. They may not be ready [to become the next leader], but at least we know they have the talent" (Ferrari, pers. comm.).

Aviv noted how executives and board members alike are often reluctant to discuss leadership succession. Likewise, Gothard and Austin (2013) found that leadership succession can stir up considerable emotion, fear, and stress that often results in discomfort between boards and executives. Aviv said the "safest way" to begin this conversion with the board is to "say 'what if the executive was run over by a bus or stricken with the most catastrophic disease, and you are in the emergency room. So what do you do then?' So you can say to them that they need to put on a piece of paper five executives who can temporarily run the organization" (Aviv, pers. comm.).

While the initial conversations with board members related to leadership succession may have been tense, all three of the organizations were able to institutionalize this management process as a board responsibility and function. Thus, the organizational leader was no longer placed in the awkward role of having to pick his or her successor.

Leadership Competencies

The executives interviewed stressed the importance of spending considerable time with board members discussing the right mix of skills needed to lead their particular organization.

"Agency leaders are often selected for the wrong reasons," Aviv said. "They may be a hell of a fundraiser, gave a fabulous speech, or were quoted in the *New York Times* five times, so everyone knows who they are. They may be fabulous and dynamic, but they are not operational leaders."

The ability to effectively manage the operations of the organization was described by the executives interviewed as including effective board management, understanding and making the greatest use of economies of scale, consistently meeting the organization's outcomes, personnel management, and maximizing the use of cost-saving technology. These competencies need to be balanced with the ability to "cast a vision" for the organization shared by board members and employees alike.

One of the key areas where effective nonprofit executives demonstrate their visionary abilities pertains to catching up to propriety firms in the initiation of commonly used technological devices in service delivery strategies. "You and I already use mobile technology to order groceries, buy books, movies, do our banking, yet we still require patients to drive to hospitals for most of their healthcare needs," Tyson said. "Basically we ask our patients to step out of the twenty-first century and go back to the twentieth century for healthcare" (Tyson, pers. comm.).

Despite the impact a sluggish economy has had on nonprofits, the executives interviewed were committed to "securing the necessary resources" to "adequately compensate" key organizational leaders (Ferrari, pers. comm.). Ferrari provided the following example with regard to one of Heifer's more recent executive-level hirings to illustrate this point:

> Civil society and nonprofit degrees underpay relative to for-profit organizations. I think that's ridiculous because incentives matter. And don't think you will be attracting the smartest people if you don't make this commitment. For example, our board [at Heifer] was only committed to paying our country director in Haiti between $60,000 and $70,000. Well, the compensation for running a three-million-dollar program was really in the range of $130,000 to $140,000. I informed the board that we were better off shutting down the program if we weren't able to hire the right talent to execute quality services. Ultimately, we were able to hire this brilliant guy and pay him $130,000. He's able to leverage the amount of money we commit to the program, so he's worth what we compensate him.

Values

In addition to discussing the competencies needed by the next generation of nonprofit leaders, the executives interviewed discussed the importance of cultivating administrators who held values that aligned with the missions of nonprofit organizations. While Tyson noted that his for-profit counterparts in the healthcare sector "were not in it just for the money," he did emphasize that his "line of sight" had to be distinct from executives in the proprietary sector. "My shareholders are the communities, the federal government, and the public's trust at large. And so, my line of sight is very direct to that interest. It is a very different mindset, but I still run a fifty-billion-dollar business so the business discipline needs to be in place," he said (Tyson, pers. comm.).

Aviv, who stated that her commitment to social justice motivated her to embark on a public-service career, said one of the
most effective tools for "exposing students to the experience" of
working for a nonprofit involves "extended volunteer and internship opportunities."

"If you ask me to take an intern I would probably say no
unless they stay for longer than three months," Aviv said. "The
nature of the work, training involved, and getting them exposed
to all the facts requires this." She said the next generation of
leaders "need to find nonprofit work useful and meaningful . . .
they need to feel they've made difference. It's about them feel-
ing empowered—it's not about the salary they're making. If you
look at all the studies about why people love their work and stay
at jobs, it has to do with this" (Aviv, pers. comm.)

An entrepreneurial, outcome-based model needs to be
aligned with this commitment to the greater good for nonprofits to remain viable in the twenty-first century. Ferrari suggested
that Heifer's work in Vietnam served as a relevant example of
these activities:

> One of the more interesting experiences for me was to
> be in a government office in Vietnam, which was a part of
> the massive resistance on the part of the North Vietnamese
> against U.S. government forces. Sitting there in the govern-
> ment offices with hammer and sickle flags everywhere, pic-
> tures of Ho Chi Minh . . . and you're talking about market
> development. And they're funding half the projects because
> they believe in what we do with economies of scale, and the
> speed in which we do our work. From their perspective,
> which is ironic coming from communists, we can mobi-
> lize communities much better than they do. (Ferrari, pers.
> comm.)

Diversity

A board that makes the shift from a culture of unplanned succession activities to one of succession management will address

issues such as competencies and the values base required for future executives. Another focus point of these ongoing discussions needs to be diversity. The executives interviewed articulated demographic shifts (see Chapter 1) that compelled board members to consider what type of leader would best represent their customers and constituencies well into the twenty-first century. In tandem with these changing demographics, the organizational leaders interviewed said that the next generation of leaders needed to effectively represent the changing racial and ethnic landscape of America. They had already brought to the attention of their respective boards reasons for encouraging women, as well as racial and ethnic minorities, to pursue executive-level positions, especially in light of the fact that white males continue to be overrepresented as CEOs of the largest American nonprofits. Ferrari captured the sentiment of the executives interviewed with regard to this subject:

> The first philosophical point is that it's about talent. It's not about gender or color or ethnic background. And that's important. When I first got here I wrote a mission statement about the work we do in global development—women play a central role in this. There's a lot of data and observations pointing to this key leadership role women play in developing their countries. That being said, I think my successor should probably be a woman. I will begin with that. The second piece is that this woman ought to probably come from the South—preferably not American born. This person needs to exhibit certain experiences, education, and an understanding of culture—it's not so much about culture, but it's this idea of being embedded in where the issues are. (Ferrari, pers. comm.)

Conclusion

Fostering a culture of succession management starts with the assumption that board members need to be involved in cultivating internal leaders, as well as being on the lookout for individuals outside of the organization who exhibit the skills, values, and backgrounds needed to effectively run their non-profit. As an institutionalized process, succession management prevents the chief administrator from having to bear the burden of selecting his or her successor, or forcing the board into making hasty decisions with regard choosing the next leader of their organization. All of the executives interviewed worked for non-profits that periodically presented a list of potential future executives to their board, in tandem with other administrators. This holistic, ongoing process of cultivating internal talent, as well as being on the lookout for prospective agency leaders external to the organization, was viewed as an effective means of determining who would be the next to lead their organizations.

Institutionalizing succession management within an organization also serves as a safeguard against choosing future leaders for the wrong reasons. Landing a huge donation or grant may be very impressive to certain board members, but this ability, or related high-profile attainments, is not always an indicator of proven operational leadership. Demonstrated competence in managing board operations and agency personnel, as well as the innovative use of technology, were deemed as being of equal importance to fundraising and other forms of revenue generation. In tandem with exhibiting a wide range of operational skills, the executives interviewed stressed the importance of recruiting leaders with value bases that aligned with the organization's mission.

In light of the central role executives play in the growth of their organizations, significant discussions were also held with regard to the backgrounds of potential leaders. While talent was the primary criterion for determining future leaders, the executives interviewed articulated how demographic trends warranted consideration in who would lead their organization. This selection criterion was deemed important because board members have to consider what type of leader would best represent the interests of their customers and constituencies well into the twenty-first century.

4 ⅠⅠⅠ International Differences in Nonprofit Succession Planning

KARL BESEL AND ANDREAS SCHMID

It probably comes as no surprise that nonprofits in other countries, especially our European counterparts, face similar challenges and opportunities with regard to executive succession planning. Most of these commonalities arise from similar demographic trends, as well as similar institutional structures found on both continents. This chapter compares succession planning in the United States with Germany in light of the similarities found between these countries, including the dynamic nonprofit sectors found within both countries. These commonalities have inspired American politicians, policymakers, and academics to use Germany as a model for proposed changes to a fragmented and costly healthcare system in the United States, going back as least as far as the early 1990s (Osborne and Gaebler 1992).

Despite some obvious differences, Germany is arguably very close to the United States in terms of how healthcare nonprofits are financed, as well the competitive marketplace in which they operate (Busse, Blümel, and Ognyanova 2013). Religiously affiliated nonprofits operated by Lutheran and Catholic churches in Germany compete for market share with other nonprofit, public, and for-profit hospitals. Consolidation, the formation of hospital systems, and a mix of private and statutory insurance, as well as public funding, are common trends in both hospital markets (Maier and Schmid 2009; Schmid and Ulrich 2013). These commonalities between the German and American health-care sectors, along with the substantially lower health-care costs, higher life expectancies, and lower infant mortality rates exhibited by Germany, have compelled many American policymakers and academics to use this country as a potential model for reinventing our costly and fragmented healthcare system over the past several decades (Osborne and Gaebler 1992). Indeed, many healthcare initiatives such as most recently the Patient Protection and Affordable Care Act embrace elements of the German system, including mandates for health-care coverage and competition for services between a host of public, nonprofit, and for-profit entities.

Germany experiences demographic change at a faster rate than the United States. According to World Health Organization data for 2013, the median age of the population is forty-six in Germany and thirty-seven in the United States. While the proportion of the elderly German population grows, this goes along with a dramatically shrinking workforce, from about forty-nine million people between twenty and sixty-four years of age in 2013 to a projection of somewhere between thirty-four and thirty-eight million in 2060. Overall the German population is expected to shrink considerably over the upcoming decades, suggesting a drop from today's eighty-one million inhabitants to a figure between sixty-seven and seventy-three million in 2060 (Destatis 2015).

The Study

The focus of this study is on executive succession planning within the German public and nonprofit health-care system. In many ways this chapter provides an international counterpoint to Chapter 3. The questions asked of nonprofit administrators in Chapter 3 were also asked of two experienced health-care executives (Dr. Georg Rüter and Jens-Peter Neumann) and one health-care consultant and former hospital administrator (Jan Hacker). Rüter has served as the CEO of a nonprofit Catholic hospital for the past twenty-five years, and Neumann has filled a similar position at a for-profit German hospital for five years. Hacker is the managing partner at Oberender and Partner, a consulting firm that works with nonprofit, public, and proprietary hospitals within Germany. All the interviews took place in May 2014.

Overview of the German Healthcare System

Political Scientist James Q. Wilson (1989) once described policymaking in Europe as being like a "prize fight," where a particular policy is implemented and typically experiences considerable longevity once legislation is passed. In contrast to this "clear winner" notion, Wilson observed that policymaking in the United States is more like a "bar room brawl" where legal battles often transpire between the federal and state governments, as well as between private citizens and the government, long after the implementation of a public policy. Thus, instead of embracing a clear-winner approach in policy making, Wilson said "policy making is never over" in the United States. Wilson's astute observation is especially poignant with regard to the comparison between the American and German health-care systems. Contentious and perpetually adversarial health-care debates have raged in the United States for decades. This is starkly contrasted with the story of the German health-care system. Essentially the basic framework for Germany's current universal health-care system was initiated by the Health Insurance Act of 1883. This seminal piece of legislation, enacted under prime minister Otto von Bismark, was designed as mandatory health insurance that applied only to low-income, blue-collar workers and certain government employees, but has since gradually been expanded to cover about 90 percent of the population. This act continues to shape the roles of payers, insurance or sickness funds, and providers, physicians, and hospitals within Germany (Solsten 1995). Over the past decades, financial pressure has increased the frequency of political interventions, making it sometimes difficult for the players in the market to adapt to a constantly changing environment (Oberender and Zerth 2010; Busse, Blümel, and Ognyanova 2013).

Demographic and Employment Trends

Demographic trends in Western European countries, including an aging workforce and relatively low birth rate, would seem to compel board members and organizational administrators to place a greater emphasis on succession planning (Leyhausen 2009). These trends, combined with the European practice of early retirement, seem to foster a perfect storm of intermingling factors that would induce agency leaders to focus more on this subject. Overall, the economic crises that have hit western societies over the last decades have led to massive waves of early retirement. This cost-cutting strategy has created a situation where the actual average retirement age is therefore much lower than the formal retirement age. Germany is a good case in point. Despite a formal retirement age of sixty-five, average retirement was around sixty years old during the 1990s (Dorn and Sousa-Poza 2004). A representative study conducted in 2002 found that around 40 percent of German firms did not employ a single worker older than fifty years of age (Backes-Gellner and Schneider 2012). Although this may appear to be an extreme example, comparative analysis points to similar developments in other European countries (Fourage and Schillis 2009).

While workers have been encouraged to retire early in Germany and other European countries over the last couple of decades, this situation is gradually changing. Not only has early retirement become too expensive for the social security system, but as baby boomers are nearing retirement, skilled workers will also become rare and the productivity potential of older employees will be needed for organizations to remain competitive. Subsequently, public policies on early retirement have started to reverse in European countries such as Denmark, which is discussing an increase in the official retirement to seventy years (Backes-Gellner and Schneider 2012).

Views on Succession Planning

In general, the German executives interviewed did not view executive succession planning with the same degree of importance as their American counterparts. The idea of actively discussing the inevitable departure of an organizational leader was deemed impolite by the interviewees. The views of the executives interviewed on this subject were captured by Hacker:

> To tell you the truth, I don't see anything like this [executive succession planning] in Germany. I know quite a significant number of public and nonprofit hospital administrators and hospital owners. It's like succession planning is considered something like dying to them. Everybody knows it's going to happen sometime, but you don't talk about it. And to address this with an existing CEO is considered to be bad manners if it happens earlier than twelve months before his retirement. I know a very successful CEO of a public hospital who is kind of married to his hospital, and just turned seventy with no intention of leaving. Although he's seventy, the board has yet to have a discussion about his succession. In order to implement succession planning, there would have to be a cultural change with this issue. (Hacker, pers. comm.)

It's important to clarify that while there seemed to be a cultural taboo with regard to executive succession planning, leadership training opportunities were discussed extensively by the interviewees. Rüter said "we spend a lot of money and quite a lot of time training all of our so-called middle management team" so they can potentially be promoted as upper administrators retire or leave. These regular training sessions included not only current managers, but also clinical staff members such as experienced doctors and nurses who demonstrate leadership potential (Rüter, pers. comm.). Essentially, succession planning was viewed in a broader sense as "leadership training" because an intentional focus on finding a replacement for an executive position was deemed impolite at best.

A recent study (KPMG 2014) points out that today the

probability that there are changes in the executive board of a German hospital is fifty times higher than in the executive board of a German company listed in the DAX Performance Index. Compared to the United States, where a hospital CEO turnover rate of twenty percent in 2013 was considered a record high (American College of Healthcare Executives 2015), the average German rate of twenty-six percent for the years 2010 to 2012 seems to be fairly high. This is primarily driven by a rate of thirty-two percent turnover in the private for-profit hospital sector, followed by twenty-five percent in the private not-for-profit sector and twenty percent in public hospitals. While turnover rates seem to be closely linked to hospitals' financial distress or lack thereof, the high turnover rates in private hospital administration may also be partly due to the aforementioned leadership training. In large hospital chains there is some routine in rotating CEOs between hospitals for their personal development (KPMG 2014).

The homogenous nature of the healthcare sector in Germany fosters an environment where the external recruitment of proven administrators can be performed with relative ease when compared with other industries, as stated by current hospital executive and former investment banker Neumann. "Everyone knows each other since this sector is ninety-nine percent domestic," he said. "This is very different from investment banking, where the field is very international."

Another leadership-planning observation made by the executives was that the church-based nonprofit hospitals seemed more effective than the public sector in succession planning "since they didn't have to look after voters with regard to salaries for nurses and other employees" (Neumann, pers. comm.). Thus, these nonprofit hospitals that were not constrained by the political process were able to focus on long-term organizational leadership strategies to a greater extent than their public counterparts.

While executive-level succession planning was generally not viewed as a subject that warranted increased attention, recruiting talented young people to assume leadership positions within hospitals was deemed to be a viable organizational pursuit.

Values

The executives interviewed discussed how hospitals seeking top talent for administrative positions typically promote the "values-based" mission and purpose of their organizations.

"I think younger people may not think that a hospital is a sexy place to work" Rüter said. "According to a recent article, four of the five favorite German companies were all in the automotive industry" (Rüter, pers. comm.). Hacker discussed how middle managers perceive "the public and nonprofit sector as being on the retreat in the current economy" (Hacker, pers. comm.).

In light of these perceptions, the executives used phrases such "Christian values," "less pressure driven," and "collaborative" to discuss how their organizations exhibited a comparative recruitment advantage over Volkswagen, BMW, or even a for-profit hospital. In addition to these values and characteristics that make public and nonprofit hospitals appealing places to work, the executives also discussed how they valued entrepreneurialism and innovation in prospective young administrators. A primary driving force behind the emphasis executives place on these qualities is the trend toward privatization of hospitals.

"Germany currently has the largest percentage of privately owned hospitals in Europe, and probably a higher percentage of for-profit hospitals than even the United States," according to Hacker (Hacker, pers. comm.). Thus, the executives viewed the next generation of administrators as needing to exhibit business savvy in the increasingly competitive healthcare marketplace while remaining true to a core set of personal values.

Competencies

The wide array of healthcare providers and private insurance companies certainly provided the United States with a model for healthcare reform legislation. Nonetheless, the executives interviewed perceived American nonprofit and public hospitals as responding to changes in the marketplace with greater ease and efficiency than in Germany.

"German hospitals still operate in a more regulated manner and don't have the same commitment to the consumer as American hospitals," Rüter said (Rüter, pers. comm.). The interviewees said the next generation of German health-care executives will need to implement more customer-driven organizational strategies. In addition to operating in a nimbler fashion within an evolving marketplace, the executives interviewed deemed "effective board management" and "personnel management" as primary competencies that administrators were required to possess. In many ways, these conversations were quite similar to the ones held with American executives. Twenty years [ago] when I started in this position, I spent most of my time with the economics side of managing a hospital," Rüter said. "Now I spend at least seventy percent of my time with personnel issues. These include attracting employees, hiring, and firing, as well as personality problems and leadership development. We still need to do more [as administrators] in personnel development. That's OK . . . it's a nice job, and it makes me happy to see young people developing their leadership skills" (Rüter, pers. comm.).

Conclusion

Many Americans (and unfortunately quite a few politicians) continue to view health care in Europe as "socialized medicine" where health care is rationed, and thus is seen as inferior to American health care, mainly due to an absence of competition. This chapter illustrates that German hospitals probably have more in common with their American counterparts than it seems, including a large percentage of church-owned nonprofits, as well as a growing number of proprietary hospitals. While this competitive marketplace serves to foster efficiencies and exemplary health-care outcomes when compared to the United

States, the executives interviewed suggested that most German hospitals exhibited limitations with regard to customer service. They believed that the next generation of hospital administrators would need to exhibit greater levels of entrepreneurship and a willingness to innovate than is found in current hospital executives. These competencies will be required as the historically generous German welfare state will inevitably face continued cutbacks. Subsequently, nonprofit and public health-care providers will experience increased competition from a growing number of for-profit hospitals. Similar to the nonprofit and public sectors in the United States, health-care mergers and acquisitions have become more frequent (Schmid and Ulrich 2013).

In light of the dynamic and rapidly changing marketplaces in which German hospitals operate, one would expect a greater emphasis would be placed on executive succession planning. The literature review and interviews discussed in this study reveal that the opposite is true. A combination of factors, including a gradual reversal of early retirement policies, as well as cultural and social taboos surrounding discussions about a key leader leaving an organization, has resulted in a virtual nonexistence of this practice by German public and nonprofit hospitals. That being said, a growing emphasis is being placed on leadership development.

Along with conversations about an executive's inevitable departure being perceived as rude or impolite, the use of terms such as leadership or personnel development workshops and retreats were perceived as being more palatable to current executives and board members alike. The utilization of these activities for growing the number of internal leaders was viewed as being fairly comprehensive within many German hospitals.

5 ||| Succession Planning and Foundations

CHARLOTTE LEWELLEN WILLIAMS AND KARL BESEL

The Center on Community Philanthropy at the Clinton School of Public Service is dedicated to researching, teaching, writing, and learning about community philanthropy as an approach to delivering public service. The center functions much like a non-profit organization in that it is a special unit within the school that receives grants from local and national funders to support its work within the state and Delta region. During my (Charlotte Lewellen Williams') time as director of the center, I have experienced the transition in leadership at several national foundations from the perspective of both a grantee and an outside observer. I have been intrigued to watch how large philanthropic institutions handle succession planning and interested in their approach to avoiding some of the challenges that foundations often face when a CEO leaves the organization. These issues are relevant for foundations because even though there is growing recognition by institutions of the importance of succession planning, only a small number have formalized practices in place for accomplishing this goal (Gothard and Austin 2013; Austin and Salkowitz 2009; Bell, Moyers, and Wolfred 2006). Often governing boards anticipate that the executive director will lead the process of planning for his or her successor even though it is well documented in the literature that boards have final accountability for succession planning (Bell, Moyers, and Wolfred 2006; Dalton and Dalton 2007.

Changing demographics in the overall workforce population and implications for nonprofit leadership should also be highlighted in the discussion of succession planning and foundations. It is projected that in the next fifteen years, minorities will be more than fifty percent of all entrants into the workforce. By the year 2050, thirty percent of the population of the United States will be members of minority groups, with the fastest growing minority cohorts being Latinos and Asians. In 2002, Independent Sector, a national nonprofit and philanthropy membership organization, found that the nonprofit sector employs a higher proportion of African Americans and a lower proportion of Latinos compared to both the public and private sectors. The nonprofit sector workforce is about 82 percent Caucasian, 10 percent African American, 5 percent Latino, 3 percent other, and 1 percent Asian or Pacific Islander. Most leadership positions are still held by whites—between 75 percent and 84 percent, with 10 percent held by African Americans, 6 percent by Asians, and 4 percent by Latinos (Halpern 2006).

Gender, specifically gender diversity in nonprofit leadership, is also an issue to consider with succession planning. The nonprofit sector has a higher proportion of female employees compared to the total population of women in the American workforce, 68 percent compared to 46 percent. Women made up the majority of nonprofit executive directors, but in only smaller organizations. Men lead 40 percent of nonprofit organizations, but 55 percent of organizations with budgets greater than five million dollars. Moreover, women are typically paid less than men (Halpern 2006).

An interesting note is that grantmakers such as the David and Lucile Packard Foundation, the San Francisco Foundation, and the Evelyn and Walter Hass Jr. Fund have joined the Annie E. Casey Foundation in assisting nonprofits with succession planning and leader vacancies (Hall 2006). In this chapter we explore whether select foundations have taken the advice of their peer organizations regarding leadership departures and if they are actively promoting succession planning within their own organizations. We also seek to understand some of the influencing factors that lead these foundation executives into a life of public service and what their views are on motivating the next generation of philanthropy leaders.

Study Design

The focus of this chapter is on executive succession planning within foundations and other philanthropic institutions. This chapter provides a comparative view of how foundation executives perceive succession planning from the standpoint of both their own organizations and their personal insights as public servants. Three CEO-level leaders of major American foundations—Dr. Sherece West, Sterling Speirn, and Ron Carpenter—were interviewed and the same questions presented to them as previous respondents in Chapters 2 and 3. West is the president and CEO of the Winthrop Rockefeller Foundation in Little Rock, Arkansas. Speirn led the W. K. Kellogg Foundation in Battlecreek, Michigan, as its president from 2006 to 2013. Carpenter is the president and CEO of Indiana State University Foundation in Terre Haute, Indiana. All the interviews were conducted October 2013 and June 2014.

The View from Foundations

Leadership transitions at foundations are often viewed as important and anticipated, but rarely are they seen as smooth, well-planned conversions from one CEO to the next. Donna Stark, director of leadership development at the Annie E. Casey Foundation, said "succession planning is so important, but no one is doing it." A national survey of 2,200 executive directors commissioned by the Casey Foundation found more than half of the organizations surveyed had no succession plan, even though nearly two-thirds of the executives planned to leave their jobs by 2009. The Greater Kansas City Community Foundation found this trend to be even higher, reporting that 86 percent of nonprofit groups in the Kansas City, Missouri, area lacked succession plans (Hall 2006). In 2011, the Meyer Foundation published a report that surveyed three thousand nonprofit and foundation executive directors regarding succession planning and found that only 17 percent had a succession plan in place (Cornelius, Moyers, and Bell 2011).

While some philanthropic institutions have studied the lack of succession planning within the nonprofit sector, others have identified additional challenges impacting leadership transition, such as retiring baby boomers and dwindling replacement prospects among their colleagues. The retiring of baby boomers is well-documented as an issue of concern for the next wave of nonprofit leadership, including foundation presidents. Statistics show that elected officials and nonprofit leaders reaching age sixty-five will increase steadily over the next decade to more than four million by the year 2020 (Census Bureau 2012). Filling these positions with qualified, well-trained individuals will be a challenge for the sector. Complicating this issue is the low likelihood that these exiting leaders will be replaced with executives from within their own organizations. A study of about two thousand nonprofit leaders conducted by the Eugene and Agnes E. Meyer Foundation found that only about a third of charity leaders report that they currently have identified senior officers within their organizations who are skilled and willing to take over the top executive job (Hall 2006). This implies that the majority of nonprofit organizations with exiting CEOs are not confident that they will locate a replacement from among their ranks. These issues point to a need for formalized succession planning to deal with the inevitable wave of change in nonprofit leadership.

Promoting from Within

Cultivating leadership from within was a theme repeated across interview responses. "Succession planning is—and I'm talking specifically about foundations now—it's unfortunate that big private foundations are notorious for not going inside and not even staying inside the field," Speirn said. "So many CEOs at big private foundations don't come from philanthropy, they come from academia, they come from government, they come from business. It's almost as if, 'you can work really hard here but when it comes to a leadership position we need other people.'" (Speirn, pers. comm.).

In a notable exception, in 2013, The W. K. Kellogg Foundation announced its new president and CEO as LaJune Montgomery Tabron, who had previously held the position of Chief Financial Officer and had been with the organization for more than twenty years.

"When I leave here I believe we have a succession plan at WRF . . . and if God forbid something negative happened to me, I believe we definitely have a staff, a team, who can temporarily be put in place until the next steps are had," West said. "Ideally I'd love to see our vice president or our Chief Operating Officer become the next CEO of WRF, because I believe that in terms of leadership, they can do this job. . . . So in terms of my responsibility in making sure that we have a solid bench, I have done that part" (West, pers. comm.).

While atypical, there are other examples of foundations that have promoted internal candidates to the top job, such as the David and Lucile Packard Foundation, which appointed Carol Larson to president and CEO in 2004, and the Ford Foundation's appointment of Darren Walker to president and CEO in 2014. The W. K. Kellogg Foundation, the David and Lucile Packard Foundation, and the Ford Foundation are three philanthropic institutions whose willingness to promote internal candidates to lead their organizations is potentially a step toward reducing obstacles in succession planning.

In light of the pivotal role played by members of the board of directors in fundraising and policy development, foundations may want to take a broader scope in identifying potential leaders; volunteer leaders are often viable candidates for these positions. When the Indiana State University Foundation was scrambling to secure a new leader following the abrupt departure of the organization's chief administrator, it considered members of its board of directors as potential candidates. Carpenter, an Indiana State University Foundation board member who also happened to be to be the head of the Indiana State Alumni Association, was quickly spotted as a viable candidate for the job.

"My volunteer leadership experience in higher education, relationship capital in the community, along with my thirty-five years of experience in the child-welfare field allowed the board to vet me quickly for this position," Carpenter said. While he viewed his experience as the CEO of a large social-service agency as being "similar" in many ways to his current role as a university foundation president, he emphasized some key distinctions in holding chief leadership positions between the two fields.

"As a social service administrator you spend a lot of time securing and maintaining governmental contracts," he said. "As a foundation president you are constantly out in the community raising dollars, as well as securing community revenues and assets. It's a different skill set, and hopefully foundations have plans for growing talent internally to fill these leadership positions" (Carpenter, pers. comm.).

Board Development

Diversity, training, and overall board development were also mentioned by the executives interviewed as important facets of successful succession planning. "we did board training, especially with Board Source and the Center for Effective Philanthropy," West said. "They talk about strategic planning, visioning, succession planning, you know, basically a board's best practice, a succession plan is included in a board's best practice. Our organizations are holding our nonprofits to a standard but we also have to meet that standard, and so it became important that we were doing best policies and best practices internally. And succession planning is one of those best practices" (West, pers. comm.).

"We're not on automatic pilot . . . we have a more coherent

culture about what we're trying to achieve as a foundation, not as four different departments looking all over the world, and so that's not a bad business model either if you say 'that's how we work'," said Speirn.

Interviewees discussed the value of diversity in the context of recruiting qualified, experienced executives for foundation leadership transition and as a component of board development. "It's not easy to recruit people to a small town in Western Michigan," Speirn said. "They could go anywhere in the country to do their work. You have to have something special here to get people to come here as well as an agenda and a culture that really values difference and doesn't want people to show up and be like everybody else" (Speirn, pers. comm.)

West said boards do not need to worry about hurting feelings when doing succession planning:

> A board really needs to be prepared, stop worrying about offending the CEO because this is being discussed . . . just get on putting a good plan in place. It's really the board's responsibility, not a CEOs responsibility, to put a succession plan in place. That is a board function. In some organizations, CEOs have no say in who succeeds them, so when you talk about diversity, again that depends on the organization. When I left an organization they asked me to find my replacement and to make recommendations, but it was ultimately up to the board to make that selection. (West, pers. comm.)

Carpenter also discussed how boards assume succession planning as a primary responsibility, but emphasized the importance of "CEOs in recruiting competent board members that understand what succession planning entails." He went on, "sophistication makes a world of difference in board development. Smaller organizations typically have a limited number of board members, and often their schedules aren't as flexible. They are also lucky if their organization's leader gives them a thirty-day notice with regard to leaving the agency" (Carpenter, pers. comm.).

Next-Generation Public Service Leaders

To address the matter of nonprofit leaders retiring from their jobs and the potential shortage of their replacements, we asked the executives what can be done to help motivate young people toward careers in public service. Speirn said America needs to educate all its citizens to fulfill the promise of American democracy:

> I think all jobs bring meaning and value. I went through college and law school working hard-labor construction jobs, mowing lawns, painting houses. I was a paperboy. I was a member of the North Carolina bar without a job— throwing the *Durham Morning Herald* seven days a week. But I think now more than ever, certainly in my lifetime, in terms [of] a young person coming out for a mid-career, wanting to make a difference, our country is, certainly not for the first time, at a perilous crossroads. Not educating 30 to 40 percent of our kids, falling behind on the world stage and globalization, and we're the longest-living democracy on the planet, right? We have amazing freedoms that other people don't. We have amazing material abundance that enables us to—and yet we are not living up to—the promise and aspirations, I think, that our founders had dreamed for. Having a democracy for good citizens who want to participate and have good livelihoods to take care of their families. So I think the fact the challenge of this country delivering on its promise and what it means to be a member of this society has never been more critical. And public service is the most direct way to attend to that. (Speirn, pers. comm.)

West said it's important to see service as a calling.

I would say that being of service to your friends, family, citizens, neighborhoods, communities, is what we're really called to do period. Now that has a lot of spiritual undertones to it, and I'm not ashamed to say that it does, and in any capacity that you can contribute to ensuring that the systems that impact children and families work well, then please contribute to it. We have young people who are in foster care and we need leaders who will make that system of care as efficient and effective as possible. We have folk who are in elder care in some stage, Medicare, Medicaid. We need all of those systems to function. We need excellent leadership. We need qualified, visionary, strategic leaders to ensure that those who are recipients of those services get the absolutely best service we can provide. (West, pers. comm.)

Conclusion

Philanthropy is a term often reserved for grand institutions, large endowments, or large donations. Rarely is philanthropy seen as an *approach* to public service. In general, nonprofit organizations tend to view economic and community development through the lens of state and federal grants. Philanthropy, and sometimes voluntary service, is often disregarded in such development models and seen by many as one class giving to another: external investment from the outside in.

Since the creation of the Clinton School Center on Community Philanthropy, perceptions are beginning to shift toward viewing philanthropy as a powerful tool to transform communities from within toward a fully recognized culture of generosity aimed at social and economic equity. This paradigm shift requires a renewed commitment to identify, cultivate, and grow strong visionary leaders to guide the philanthropic and nonprofit sector. Is it possible to thread together strategies for succession planning at foundations, with recent trends in foundation leadership transitions (promoting from within) and create a motivation map that helps invigorate next generation leaders to look toward philanthropy as a fulfilling career in public service? Interviewees in this chapter suggest the answer could be yes. Building the pool of candidates for next-generation foundation leadership by targeting talent within the philanthropy sector is a potential solution with promise.

6 ▮▮▮ Mergers, Acquisitions, and Leadership in Health-Care Succession Planning

ADAM R. SMITH

All organizations must be able to adapt to change. The capacity to change and the level of readiness for change are vital for all organizations in the increasingly interconnected and evolving global environment we live in today. One area of uncertainty for organizations can be the development of leadership within the organization. Additionally, the organizations that will be the focus of this chapter also have to deal with the challenges and complexities of the health-care field. Health care is the focus of this chapter because of the above-average growth projected in management positions in this area.

While the specific examples in this chapter are drawn from a number of hospitals, the perspectives shared are applicable to the broader health-care field. Throughout this chapter are examples that are in fact generalizable to the larger public-service sector as well. This book aims to show readers the view from the corner office; in this chapter the examples happen to be from small, rural hospitals.

The main challenge discussed in this chapter relates to how leaders in the public-service sector will plan for the transitional period that is already underway as baby boomers retire in droves. The key topic in this regard is succession planning. Succession planning is important to all organizations because they must ensure that they have the necessary knowledge, skills, and abilities present in the firm in order to set themselves up for success. Succession planning is not just another human resource management activity that requires monthly or yearly paperwork completion. It must be sold at every level of management. Top management team commitment is of the utmost importance. Another vital aspect of successful succession planning is buy-in from the board of directors.

A more specific focus of this chapter will be leadership succession planning. Leadership succession planning in organizations is essentially the process of matching leadership skills with company needs. This is an area of great importance that can have an impact on employee morale, organizational climate, turnover, commitment, and satisfaction.

Additionally, this chapter will discuss how the view from the corner office of several hospitals can be altered by special challenges presented by such added variables as the involvement of the board of directors and the threat and pressure of mergers and acquisitions.

Leadership succession planning should not be taken lightly. This is easy to say from an academic standpoint, but in a number of areas there can be a disconnect between theory and practice, between research and application, between ideals and the realities of doing business in today's climate. Therefore, it's not as if one is going to find an abundance of existing literature that argues against succession planning at leadership levels in the public-service sector (or more specifically here, health care); however, a great deal of health-care-related literature only offers theoretical views of best practices. Thus, the intent here is to profile the view from the corner office of several hospitals, and extrapolate to the broader health-care field and public-service sector.

In health care, even for nonprofits, the organization must operate with the same concerns as private-sector enterprises. And it comes down to time and money. The concern in this chapter is that smaller organizations may perceive a lack of resources related to succession planning (Ip and Jacobs 2006). The majority of nonprofit organizations are considered small, and therefore do not usually even have the ability to support two top executives (Froelich, McKee, and Rathge 2011). It has also been noted that "few companies seem to have the time, the luxury, or the patience to grow CEOs anymore" (Byrne, Reingold, and Melcher 1997).

Choosing the successor used to be the privilege and obligation of the outgoing chief executive officer, but now that onus is on the board of directors. However, the board of a small nonprofit hospital is typically preoccupied with the mere survival of the organization. Within this context, "companies should think twice about spending a lot of time and money on someone who may walk out of the door anyway. A healthier attitude today may be to consider the world as your bench" (Byrne, Reingold, and Melcher 1997). Roughly fifty years ago, companies rarely looked to external recruitment to replace the CEO, but this time has long passed, as more than one-third of large corporations now find their CEOs from talents pools outside of the company. Thus, the recruitment of talent from outside the organization will come up as a point of emphasis later in this chapter.

So while succession planning plays an important role in many sectors, one may be thinking "What does it look like in the health-care field?" The data show that 55 percent of American hospitals have some sort of succession planning program in place, up from only 21 percent of hospitals a mere ten years ago (Collins 2009). But there is still a long way to go to get anywhere close to the 93 percent of private-sector organizations in the United States that already had established a formal succession plan twenty years ago (Flynn 1995).

Leadership succession planning in small, nonprofit hospitals appears to occur at an even lower rate. But why is that? Is the board afraid to pass control of the organization to the next generation? Surely not, as they are not replacing themselves. Therefore, it must be an issue of planning, politics, or money.

Profile: Which Corner Office is the Focus?

The experiences highlighted in this chapter come from the viewpoint of the CEO, and amount to almost twenty years of experience at the helm of four different hospitals. An interview was conducted in late 2014 with Jerome Horn, who served as CEO of four small, rural hospitals in Alabama, Florida, Indiana, and Virginia before his retirement. In a career that spanned almost thirty years in hospital administration, he also served in director of finance, comptroller, and chief financial officer roles prior to moving to the corner office. And as will become a theme shortly, he did so as an external hire for each hospital as his career advanced. This is a profile of one CEO, but it represents case studies from those four hospitals spread out across the United States.

Horn said that half to two-thirds of the around 4,800 hospitals in the United States would fall into the small hospital category, and of those, 80 percent are public, non-profit community hospitals like the ones where he worked. His perspective speaks to that experience.

Tales from Four Hospitals: What Lessons Can Be Learned from Small, Rural Hospitals?

Horn worked as a CFO at a hospital in Pennsylvania for two years before being recruited by the board chairman at the first hospital where he had worked in Indiana to become its CEO.

The consensus in the field of human resources is that leadership succession can be accomplished via the use of search firms, internal development, or interim CEOs. Froelich, McKee, and Rathge (2011) found that few nonprofit organizations have strategic plans for leadership succession.

"If you were fortunate you might have a number two, a COO, that might be responsible for all [the] other ancillary areas" of the hospital, Horn said, but the first hospital he worked for "had a number two, an assistant administrator, but that was the first position cut" when belt-tightening was needed. "You look at the smaller hospitals today and you don't have a number two just waiting in the wings to take over for the CEO," he said. Leadership planning at small hospitals is often focused on external processes rather than cultivating internal candidates. "What these smaller hospitals did in terms of succession planning was strictly rely on either recruiting firms to identify candidates for them, or the hospital association," Horn said (Horn, pers. comm.).

Leadership Planning: When Should Organizations Recruit from Outside?

Horn said there was one way internal leadership development could take place at small hospitals like the ones he ran.

"Sometimes what I found is that I could bring someone [in] . . . from the banking industry . . . if you could identify a strong management person you can sort of cultivate them to take over some of the ancillary departments," he said. "And that's the extent primarily of succession planning that I saw happening in these smaller hospitals where I worked" (Horn, pers. comm.). So in order to even come close to succession planning internally, there was first a need to find talent outside the organization to fill a role a step or two below the CEO.

While other areas within the hospital may have plans to replace their ranks using internal sources, this does not always appear to be the case with top brass. One example in the healthcare field would be nursing. There is an abundance of literature on succession planning in nursing, with the goal of eventual movement up to the chief nursing officer positions. Along those lines, Horn said, "within the departments you can see mentoring and grow[ing] potential and cultivating people that may be able to replace a department manager, but you didn't see a lot of it at the senior management level." Horn said he saw planning: "within the nursing group and the department managers within their expertise, like radiology and the lab. There was a lot of that and there was a lot of grooming the next department manager but it didn't go much beyond that" (Horn, pers. comm.).

Individual departments may plan to replace retiring baby boomers, for example, but this same philosophy is not always applied to leadership succession planning.

At the senior level, Horn said succession planning in small, rural hospitals was "pretty much nonexistent. If you lost a senior manager you went outside to the hospital association or the professional placement [services]." The importance of leadership succession planning appears to be evident to hospital leadership, but the real concern, as Horn said, was fiscal.

"We had board retreats where we discussed personnel and we would discuss the potential for the CEO to not be there, what we would do if something happened to the CEO," he said. "But there was just not enough money to bring someone in to cultivate into that role" (Horn, pers. comm.). It does not seem to be an issue of planning or politics, at least not in the hospitals that are part of this case study, but rather the crux of the matter is money. However, something in the process needs to change, as the projected growth in health-care management positions continues, and the approaching retirement of baby boomers only amplifies the problem.

At one of the hospitals discussed by Horn, the CEO succession process unfolded in the following way: "I went in as an interim [CEO] and they told me they would be more than happy to consider me for the position." After he left his interim role, "they put another interim in that was part of the health care and management team from the health-care district" after which they found someone through the hospital association. "There was nobody in line that could take the job over [at] the hospital." Another hospital where Horn served as CEO had the same problem with a lack of internal development. After he left the hospital, "they used the director of HR for about six months as interim," he said. "Again, they never considered him for the position" (Horn, pers. comm.).

How can hospitals, health-care organizations, and the larger public sector handle this trend toward external recruitment? Ultimately, this requires the board of directors to play an ever-increasing role in leadership succession planning. However, is it sustainable to always focus on recruiting external talent, or will the culture and mindset in public-sector organizations need to change and evolve?

The theme of monetary constraints influencing the process came up again when Horn said, "I've seen it happen in these small hospitals, when someone is going to retire and they know they are going to retire, they wait until the person is gone and then start the process." So even with advanced information that indicates a definite need for succession, the board was either unable or unwilling to start the replacement process ahead of time, most likely because of budget constraints.

Horn said most of the time spent at board retreats was focused on keeping the hospital afloat rather than succession planning, but given the numbers that's not a good strategy.

"In health care and hospitals over the last thirty years, the average turnover of hospital CEOs across the United States has been in the 15 to 20 percent range," Horn said. "That tells you that CEO positions turnover about every five to seven years, and as hospitals struggle that can be even higher" (Horn, pers. comm.).

Succession Planning: How are Organizations Prepared for the Future?

Even if it is not apparent at the senior management level, small glimmers of hope relating to succession planning at lower levels of the organization are sometimes visible.

"There was the movement towards customer satisfaction [that] became extremely important," Horn said. "That movement did encourage the smaller hospitals to look within to find employees that could take on supervisory-type roles. There was a strong effort for that. That helped us in terms of trying to find and groom people to be department managers. We started doing rotating managers on call and we rotated it through the senior-management group, so that gave people a little better understanding of the overall operations."

Managers would "come in and visit every department in the

hospital and cover all shifts for that weekend . . . it was amazing the feedback that I got from those people that had never worked in [another area]," he said. "It really strengthened the overall organization. That's the kind of thing you would try to use for succession planning."

Money problems at hospitals do not just have to do with salaries, he continued.

"One of the other things that went away . . . they usually had really good tuition-reimbursement programs, but again when cost cutting started, that's one of the first things that you eliminated or reduced significantly," Horn said. "So you didn't have the ability to groom someone through obtaining a higher degree." It is worth noting that similar constraints from all directions will hamper planning efforts in public-service sector organizations in general.

For-profit hospitals had a different perspective on succession planning, Horn said. "They wanted the quality physicians to stay with [the] organization, but even the quality physicians, if they opposed them bringing more physicians [in] they couldn't care less because they knew they had a network and they had dedicated physician recruiters where they could go after additional physicians," he said. "In my mindset you needed to bring physicians that had an interest in your community and had an interest in living in a small, rural area. With the for-profits they would go out and find physicians that they could hire and they placed them where they wanted them" (Horn, pers. comm.). This illustrates that in public service it is of great importance to try to find talent that fits with the culture of your organization and believes in your cause. Specifically, this example points out that for-profit hospitals have additional luxuries that give them more flexibility.

It's clear from Horn's experiences, as well as from the literature, that the board plays a key role in health-care organization management.

Board Involvement: How Much Input Do Leaders Want or Need?

Research points to the board's role in leadership succession planning, but often there is no direction for them (Dalton and Dalton 2007). Either intentionally or unintentionally, the boards of small hospitals are devoting insufficient attention to the future success of the organization. This aligns with Gothard and Austin (2013), as they suggested that nonprofits generally acknowledge the importance of succession planning, but few have plans.

Horn suggested the board of directors should be focused on fundraising. "Most community not-for-profit hospital boards should be an advocate for raising money for the hospital," he said.

But there is also often a delicate political balance that comes into play in hospital boards, he said.

"The board [at the public hospital in Indiana] was appointed by the county commissioners and it was plenty political in nature," he said. "Here was the makeup of my board: I had a five-member board and . . . as long as you kept a political party in power the makeup of the board was going to be at least three Republicans and two Democrats or vice versa and then they tried within those five board appointments . . . to get geographic representation. I had on my board a manufacturing supervisor [who] was the chair, I had a farmer from the southern part of the county, I had an insurance agent from the northern part of the county, I had a college professor, and a physician."

"Boards are more active in the smaller communities and smaller hospitals and from a business standpoint that can create major problems for the operation of a facility because board members have various degrees of understanding of operating a medical facility. If they try to get involved in the day-to-day operations, they can create more problems and conflict than you can solve as a CEO. So the problem that I believe that most smaller facility CEOs have is keeping the board focused and keeping them looking at the direction of the hospital and evaluating the CEO" (Horn, pers. comm.).

It is clear that the board's role in leadership succession planning in small nonprofit hospitals is confounded by political influence, fundraising requirements, and varying degrees of expertise, much as it is in the larger health-care field and the greater public-service sector. However, according to Horn, the real concern is that "money and time [are] not there. They recognize that number one if you are going to do succession planning then you are going to move someone in that you are going to groom, there has to be a position for them. And the management structure of these smaller hospitals is so lean, that you hire people for their expertise in an area" (Horn, pers. comm.).

The biggest point of emphasis is that the board of directors at small, rural, nonprofit hospitals must focus on survival. When that concern takes precedence over all else, one option for the board is to explore mergers and acquisitions.

Mergers and Acquisitions: Another Challenge to Succession Planning

One of the limited options that small, rural hospitals have available to them to access capital is to consider mergers or acquisitions. "Smaller hospitals spend so much of their time struggling with services and how they are going to grow revenue," Horn said (Horn, pers. comm.). Hospital consolidation since 2000 has increased from 38 percent to 53 percent, and most recently to 62 percent (Lineen 2014). "Now what happens with for-profits and why they are successful when a community not-for-profit might not be nearly as successful would be they have much, much better access to capital," Horn said.

"In the small rural hospitals, the condition you run into as a CEO is your focus is on trying to keep the hospital afloat . . . and the kind of things I saw in my career at hospitals was they just struggled along and thought they were doing well if they could just break even . . . what that kept them from being able to do was to accumulate anything from capital needs and as they struggled for several years to break even or [post] small profits, they fell behind and that's what encouraged more of the merger and acquisition wave" (Horn, pers. comm.)

What changes with a strategic partner? The mission, vision, values, and goals are all subject to adjustment. In order to be successful, mergers and acquisitions require a strong integration plan and strong senior leaders (Dixon 2002). With the concerns of mergers and acquisitions in mind, the main human resources issues regarding staffing revolve around what the new practices will be in terms of organizational culture, labor practices, benefits, union relations, communication, and potential staff reduction. However, often these concerns receive little attention from the board.

The resulting organization from a merger or acquisition is a reflection of the leader. Regarding for-profit hospitals, Horn stated, "they have a much stronger planning function and they have a model they use that is very different than the community not-for-profit CEO mindset and that is everybody is expendable. They are not going to waste their money. That's typical of the small for-profit start-up industry where they bring their business model and again regardless of the community and the people that are the heart of the hospital they believe that anybody is replaceable."

Because the planning function is stronger in for-profit hospitals, there may be a greater emphasis on leadership succession planning. "From a succession planning standpoint, they [for-profit hospitals] were big enough and they had to have a corporate staff and a staff operating hospitals," Horn said. "If they, through acquisitions, could find management personnel that they could support and groom into taking over these CEO positions in the smaller hospitals, then that was an advantage for them. That was a real advantage for the for-profits."

However, the for-profit hospitals are not always successful. "In the last hospital that I served as interim CEO that was a hospital that was owned by the hospital district of [the] county and they sold their hospital to one of these for-profit hospitals for twenty-four million dollars," Horn said. "The for-profit operated the hospital for less than four years and approached the health-care district to buy it back and they sold it back to them for four million and they walked away" (Horn, pers. comm.). We did not get into any more specifics during the interview, but this example shows that for-profit hospitals are not perfect either.

While these examples are from hospitals, the themes apply to the public service-oriented sector in general, and in all broad senses of planning, the key is the need to involve staff and stakeholders from all levels in the planning process. And then more specifically, this same approach should be taken for leadership succession planning.

Conclusion: What Are the Implications for Public-Service Organizations?

While the focus of this chapter has been on the challenges faced by small, rural hospitals, the insights can be generalized outside of the health-care field. What the case study of four hospitals showed is very much in line with other research on small hospitals, and that is a virtual nonexistence of leadership succession planning in small hospitals. But this extends to other organizations. Thus, as resources only get tighter the central question remains: How can professionals from outside the organization demonstrate to small health-care organizations that leadership succession planning is worth their investment?

As competition increases in health care, the public sector and the private sector, the board of directors must come to realize that a lengthy gap in leadership at the top will hurt any competitive advantage they have established. Perhaps measurement of variables such as return on investment are needed to sell leadership succession planning to the board. Or it may be that mergers and acquisitions with for-profit health-care systems are the only way to secure the financial latitude to grow internal CEO successors. Hopefully this is not the case, but in some areas it may be the reality.

In an ideal world, organizations that realize the importance of succession planning would also have the resources (time and money) to execute needed planning. However, organizations in the public-service-oriented sector must make the best of the situation that presents itself. While small, rural, nonprofit hospitals may not be in a financial position to make substantive changes in the near future, at the very least succession planning should be a part of the CEOs yearly performance review. Once again, this applies elsewhere in the health-care field and in the public-service sector overall. Very much in line with the advice given by Santora, Caro, and Sarros (2007), the fact of the matter for small hospitals with limited resources for leadership development is that their succession planning will have to be focused on a very deliberate search for talent outside the organization.

Additionally, professional development and grooming of physicians presents an interesting twist in the health-care field. Horn said that the "key is growth, you can only grow if you increase revenue and you can only increase revenue if you add services or if you add physicians." Additionally, "today things have changed a lot and that is there [are] a lot more physicians that are moving into administrative roles and part of the reason for that is hospitals are hiring physicians now" according to Horn (Horn, pers. comm.).

The main takeaway here is that even though organizations in the public-service sector may not have the resources to keep a successor in the wings, they should still be taking advantage of human resources systems already in place. This could include, but is not limited to, compiling performance appraisal results, adding in continuing-education records, updating job descriptions, considering career-development plans, and determining if any assessment of leadership potential has been conducted. The CEO and the board of directors must view succession planning as an opportunity to improve efficiency in any organization. In the end, effective leaders will need to find ways to develop their people.

REFERENCES

Introduction

Bureau of Labor Statistics, U.S. Department of Labor. 2015. *Occupational Outlook Handbook, 2014–2015 Edition, Medical and Health Services Managers.* http//www.bls.gov/ooh/management/medical-and-health services managers.htm.

1 ▮▮▮ The State of Public Service in America

Bureau of Economic Analysis. 2001. *Nonprofit Institutions Serving Households, 2001 Report.* http://www.bea.gov/table/iTable.cfm.

Bureau of Economic Analysis. 2013. *Nonprofit Institutions Serving Households, 2013 Report.* http://www.bea.gov/table/iTable.cfm.

Census Bureau, Population Division. 2012. *Monthly Postcensal Civilian Population, by Single Year of Age, Sex, Race and Hispanic Origin.* http://www.census.gov/popest/national/asrh/2012-nat-detail.html.

Froelich, Karen, Gregory McKee, and Richard Rathge. 2011. "Succession Planning in Nonprofit Organizations." *Nonprofit Management and Leadership* 22(1): 3–20.

Herman, Robert, and Richard Heimovics. 1989. "Critical Events in the Management of Nonprofit Organizations: Initial Evidence." *Nonprofit and Voluntary Sector* Quarterly, 18(2): 119–32.

———. 1990. "The Effective Nonprofit Executive: Leader of the Board." *Nonprofit Management and Leadership:* 1(2), 167-80

———. 1994. "Executive Management and Leadership." In R.D. Herman and Associates (eds) *The Jossey-Bass Handbook of Nonprofit Leadership.* San Francisco: Jossey-Bass, 1994.

Lewellen Williams, Charlotte, Skip Rutherford, and Susan Hoffpauir. 2013. *Pathways to Racial Healing and Equity in the American South: A Community Philanthropy Strategy.* Little Rock: Center on Community Philanthropy. http://clintonschool.uasys.edu/wp-content/uploads/2013/12/Clinton-School-Compendium-2013.pdf

Newman, William, and Howard Wallender. 1978 "Managing Not-For-Profit Enterprises." *Academy of Management Review,* 7(1): 24–31.

Powell, William, and Richard Steinberg. 2006. *The Nonprofit Sector: A Research Handbook.* New Haven, CN: Yale University Press.

Rothwell, W.J. 2002. "Putting Success into your Succession Planning." *Journal of Business Strategy* 23 (May/June): 32-37.

Salamon, L.M. 1999. *Global Civil Society: Dimensions of the Nonprofit Sector.* The John Hopkins Center for Civil Society Studies, Baltimore, MD.

Singer, Audrey. 2004. *The Rise of New Immigrant Gateways.* The Living Cities Census Series. The Brookings Institution's Center on Urban and Metropolitan Policy.

Wilson, James. 1989. *Bureaucracy: What Government Agencies Do and Why They Do It.* New York: Basic Books.

Zuniga, Victor, and Ruben Hernandez-Leon. 2006. *New Destinations: Mexican Immigration in the United States.* Russell Sage Foundation.

2 ııı Politics and Public Service

Belle, Nicola. 2013. "Experimental Evidence on the Relationship between Public Service Motivation and Job Performance." *Public Administration Review,* 73(1):143–53.

Brown, Willie. 2013. Telephone interview.

Chappell, James L. 2007. "Conflict Administration for the Public Sector." *Indiana Journal of Political Science,* Winter 33: 33–40.

Coleman, Michael. 2013. Personal interview.

Dean, Lloyd. 2013. Personal interview.

Frey, Bruno S. and Reto Jegen. 2001. "Motivating Crowding Theory." *Journal of Economic Surveys* 15(5): 589–611.

Grant, Adam M. 2013. *Give and Take: A Revolutionary Approach to Success.* New York: Viking.

Hahm, Sung Deuk, Kwangho Jung, and M. Jae Moon. 2012. "Shaping Public Corporation Leadership in a Turbulent Environment." *Public Administration Review* 73(1): 178–87.

Hamilton, Lee. 2013. Personal interview.

Johnson, Kevin. 2013. Telephone interview.

McBarnes, Chris. 2013. Personal interview.

Nalbandian, John, Robert O'Neill, Jr., J. Michael Wilkes, and Amanda Kaufman. 2013. "Contemporary Challenges in Local Government: Evolving Roles and Responsibilities, Structures, and Processes." *Public Administration Review* 73(4): 567–74.

O'Riordan, J. 2013. "Public Service Motivation." *State of the Public Service Series,* Institute of Public Administration.

O'Toole, Laurence J., Jr. 1997. "Treating Networks Seriously: Practical and Research-Based Agendas in Public Administration." *Public Administration Review* 57(1): 45–52.

Paarlberg, Laurie E., and Bob Lavigna. 2010. "Transformational Leadership and Public Service Motivation: Driving Individual and Organizational Performance." *Public Administration Review* September/October, 70(5): 710–18.

Perry, James L., and Neal D. Buckwalter. 2010. "The Public Service of the Future." *Public Administration Review* 70(s1): 238–45.

Perry, James L., Annie Hondeghem, and Lois Recascino Wise. 2010. "Revisiting the Motivational Bases of Public Service: Twenty Years of Research and an Agenda for the Future." *Public Administration Review* 70(5): 681–90.

Rittel, William Horst, and Melvin Webber. 1973. "Dilemmas in a General Theory of Planning" *Policy Sciences* 4: 155–69.

Waring, Justin, Graeme Currie, and Simon Bishop. 2013. "A Contingent Approach to the Organization and Management of Public-Private Partnerships: An Empirical Study of English Health Care." *Public Administration Review* 73 (2): 313–26.

White, Leonard D. 1942. *The Future of Government in the United States: Essays in Honor of Charles E. Merriam.* Chicago: The University of Chicago Press.

3 ııı Planning for the Next Generation of Nonprofit Leaders

Austin, Michael, and Tracy Salkowitz. 2009. *Executive Development and Succession Planning: A Growing Challenge for the American Jewish Community.* New York: Jewish Funders Network.

Aviv, Diana. 2013. Personal interview.

Bell, Jeanne, Rick Moyers, and Timothy Wolfred. 2006. *Daring to Lead: A National Study of Nonprofit Executive Leadership.* Washington D.C.: Meyer Foundation/CompassPoint Nonprofit Services.

Cao, Qing, Likoebe Maruping, and Riki Takeuchi. 2006. "Disentangling the Effects of CEO Turnover and Succession on Organizational Capabilities: A Social Network Perspective." *Organization Science* 17(5): 563–76.

Dalton, Dan, and Catherine Dalton. 2007. "CEO Succession: Some Finer—and Perhaps Provocative—Points." *Journal of Business Strategy* 28(3): 6–9.

Ferrari, Pierre. 2013. Personal interview.

Froelich, Karen, Gregory McKee, and Richard Rathge. 2011. "Succession Planning in Nonprofit Organizations." *Nonprofit Management and Leadership* 22(1): 3-20.

Gothard, Suzanne, and Michael Austin. 2013. "Leadership Succession

Planning: Implications for Nonprofit Human Service Organizations."
Administration in Social Work 37(3): 272–85.

Halpern, Patrick R. 2006. "Workforce Issues in the Nonprofit Sector: Generational Leadership Change and Diversity." *American Humanities: Initiative for Nonprofit Sector Careers.*

Tyson, Bernard. 2013. Personal interview.

4 ⫿⫿⫿ International Differences in Nonprofit Succession Planning

American College of Healthcare Executives. 2015. "Hospital CEO Turnover Rate Remains Elevated." news release, May 3, 2015.

Backes-Gellner, Uschi, and Martin Schneider. 2012. "Economic Crises and the Elderly." *Gerontology* 58: 188–92.

Busse, Reinhard, Miriam Blümel, and Diana Ognyanova. 2013. *Das deutsche Gesundheitssystem. Akteure, Daten, Analysen.* Berlin: Medizinisch Wissenschaftliche Verlagsgesellschaft.

Destatis. 2015. *13. Koordinierte Bevölkerungsvorausberechnung,* Wiesbaden.

Dorn, David, and Alfonso Souza-Poza. 2004. "Motives for Early Retirement: Switzerland in an International Comparison." FAA Discussion Paper No. 99, University of Gallen.

Fourage, Didier, and Trudie Schillis. 2009. "The Effect of Early Retirement Incentives on the Training Participation of Older Workers." *Labour* 23, s1: 85–109.

Hacker, Jan 2014. Telephone interview.

KPMG. 2014. "Geschäftsführerwechsel im deutschen Krankenhaus." Berlin.

Leyhausen, Frank 2009. "An Ageing Workforce: A Major Challenge to German SMEs." *International Journal of Human Resources Development and Management* 9(2/3): 312–15.

Maier, Christian, and Andreas Schmid. 2009. "Potentiale internationaler Vergleiche im Gesundheitswesen am Beispiel von Konzentrationsprozessen im stationären Sektor." In *Gesundheitsforschung: Aktuelle Befunde der Gesundheitswissenschaften,* ed. Winand Gellner and Michael Schmöller. Baden-Baden: Nomos, 247–58.

Neumann, Jens-Peter. 2014. Telephone interview.

Oberender, Peter, and Jürgen Zerth. 2010. *Wachstumsmarkt Gesundheit,* 3rd edition. Stuttgart: Lucius & Lucius.

Osborne, David, and Gaebler, Ted. 1992. *Reinventing Government: How the Entrepreneurial Spirit is Transforming the Public Sector.* New York: Penguin Books.

Rüter, Georg 2014. Telephone interview.

Schmid, Andreas, and Volker Ulrich. 2013. "Consolidation and Concentration in the German Hospital Market: The Two Sides of the Coin." *Health Policy* 109 (3): 301–310.

Solsten, Eric 1995. *Germany: A Country Study.* Washington, D.C.: GPO for the Library of Congress.

Wilson, James. 1989. *Bureaucracy: What Government Agencies Do and Why They Do It.* New York: Basic Books.

5 ΙΙΙ Succession Planning and Foundations

Austin, Michael, and Tracy Salkowitz. 2009. *Executive Development and Succession Planning: A Growing Challenge for the American Jewish Community.* New York: Jewish Funders Network.

Bell, Jeanne, Rick Moyers, and Timothy Wolfred. 2006. *Daring to Lead: A National Study of Nonprofit Executive Leadership.* Washington D.C.: Meyer Foundation/CompassPoint Nonprofit Services.

Cao, Qing, Likoebe Maruping, and Riki Takeuchi. 2006. "Disentangling the Effects of CEO Turnover and Succession on Organizational Capabilities: A Social Network Perspective." *Organization Science* 17(5): 563–76.

Carpenter, Ron. 2013. Personal interview.

Census Bureau, Population Division. 2012. "Monthly Postcensal Civilian Population, by Single Year of Age, Sex, Race and Hispanic Origin." http://www.census.gov/popest/national/asrh/2012-nat-detail.html.

Cornelius, Marla, Rick Moyers, and Jeanne Bell. 2011. Daring to Lead 2011: A National Study of Executive Director Leadership. San Francisco, CA: CompassPoint Nonprofit Services and the Meyer Foundation.

Dalton, Dan and Catherine Dalton. 2007. "CEO Succession: Some Finer— and Perhaps Provocative—Points. *Journal of Business Strategy* 28(3): 6–9.

Gothard, Suzanne, and Michael Austin. 2013. "Leadership Succession Planning: Implications for Nonprofit Human Service Organizations." *Administration in Social Work* 37(3): 272–85.

Halpern, Patrick R. 2006. "Workforce Issues in the Nonprofit Sector: Generational Leadership Change and Diversity." *American Humanities: Initiative for Nonprofit Sector Careers.*

Hall, Holly. 2006. "Planning Successful Successions." *Chronicle of Philanthropy.* http://philanthropy.com/free/articles/v18/i06/06000601.htm.

Speirn, Sterling. 2013. Personal interview.

West, Sherece. 2014. Personal interview.

6 ||| Mergers, Acquisitions, and Leadership in Health-Care Succession Planning

Byrne, John, Jennifer Reingold, and Richard Melcher. 1997. "Wanted: A Few Good CEOs." *Business Week*, Aug. 11, 64–70.

Collins, Sandra. 2009. "Succession Planning: Perspectives of Chief Executive Officers in US Hospitals." *The Health Care Manager* 28(3): 258–63.

Dalton, Dan and Catherine Dalton. 2007. "CEO Succession: Some Finer— and Perhaps Provocative—Points." *Journal of Business Strategy* 28(3): 6–9.

Dixon, Diane. 2002. "Surviving Mergers & Acquisitions." *Health Forum Journal* 45 (2): 24–27.

Flynn, Gillian. 1995. "Succession Planning Gets Formal." *Personnel Journal* 74(1): 20.

Froelich, Karen, Gregory McKee, and Richard Rathge. 2011. "Succession Planning in Nonprofit Organizations." *Nonprofit Management and Leadership* 22(1): 3–20.

Gothard, Suzanne, and Michael Austin. 2013. "Leadership Succession Planning: Implications for Nonprofit Human Service Organizations." *Administration in Social Work* 37(3): 272–85.

Horn, Jerome. 2014. Personal interview.

Ip, Barry, and Gabriel Jacobs. 2006. "Business Succession Planning: A Review of the Evidence." *Journal of Small Business and Enterprise Development* 13(3): 326–50.

Lineen, Jason. 2014. "Hospital Consolidation: 'Safety in Numbers' Strategy Prevails in Preparation for a Value-Based Marketplace." *Journal of Healthcare Management* 59(5): 315–17.

Santora, Joseph, Mary Caro, and James Sarros. 2007. "Succession in Nonprofit Organizations: An Insider/Outsider Perspective." *SAM Advanced Management Journal* 72(4): 26–31.

INTERVIEWEES

DIANA AVIV

Diana Aviv grew up in South Africa and witnessed terrible racial conditions throughout her childhood. When she was ten years old she promised herself she would work for social justice all her life, and social justice has remained her motivation to work in the field of social good.

The former president and CEO of the Independent Sector, she is now president and CEO of Feed America, an organized network of food banks that is leading the fight against hunger in communities nationwide.

RON CARPENTER

Ron Carpenter worked in the child-welfare field for thirty-five years before being hired as the president of the Indiana State University Foundation. Prior to this position, he was the CEO of the Children's Bureau, the largest youth service bureau in Indiana. Carpenter's motivation for embarking on a career in public service includes his parents, "who were both school teachers." He also felt compelled to work with juveniles involved in the criminal justice system "after completing an internship where I worked with delinquent kids."

LLOYD DEAN

Lloyd Dean is the CEO of Dignity Health, a not-for-profit public-benefit health-care system. What motivated Dean to participate in public service was his background growing up on and off welfare and the influence of his parents. "I had very little access to healthcare . . . but [my family] was rich in faith and family values." His parents taught him to think about not only doing what you can for yourself and family, but for others and society.

PIERRE FERRARI

Pierre Ferrari is the president and CEO of Heifer International, a nonprofit whose mission is to end poverty and hunger and care for the earth. Ferrari grew up in the Belgian Congo, and in the United States began a career in business with a triple bottom line. Growing up his parents insisted one should be "committed to others as a way to live a full complete life," an idea that has stuck with him as a motivating factor in pursuing a career in social good.

JERRY HORN

Dr. Horn worked as a hospital administrator for almost thirty years in Indiana, Virginia, and Florida before joining Indiana University Kokomo as a health-care management professor. He credits his wife, a nurse, for encouraging him to become a health-care administrator. She believed her husband could make a significant contribution by combining his financial-management skills as an accountant with his "strong desire and motivation to help people."

KEVIN JOHNSON

Kevin Johnson is the mayor of Sacramento, California. Before becoming an elected official, he played in the NBA for the Phoenix Suns. During his career as a professional athlete, he was a three-time NBA all-star. Johnson's grandfather served as a significant influence with regard to his decision to embark on a career in public service. "My grandfather believed in working hard, treating people fair, and giving back to the community. It wasn't a complicated philosophy—a man with simple values."

MAYOR CHRIS MCBARNES

Chris McBarnes is the mayor of Frankfort, Indiana. As a child, McBarnes endured numerous operations because of an immune deficiency. "I truly understood how precious time is on this earth. There is work to be done." His motivation to participate in public service is to transform the legacy office holders leave behind. He wants to be remembered as a leader "who deals in public policy rather than simply a politician." He hopes to raise the bar so that future mayors are held to the same level of accountability.

STERLING SPEIRN

Sterling Speirn is the former president and CEO of the W. K. Kellogg Foundation. He attributes much of his desire to work in public service to being involved in various social issues in the 1960s. "I was raised to believe in the values of this country and commitment to equality. And the minute I got to college in the fall of 1966, every year, if not every semester or quarter, there seemed to be a new issue that challenged my belief that my country really lived up to these ideals."

BARNARD TYSON

Bernard Tyson is the Chairman and CEO of Kaiser Permanente, a not-for-profit integrated managed care consortium. His motivation to work in the sector is the opportunity to contribute to the greater good. He believes his shareholders are "the communities, the federal government, and the public's trust at large."

SHERECE WEST

Dr. Sherece West is the president and CEO of the Winthrop Rockefeller Foundation. West feels a calling and duty to be a public servant, and she believes people in the field are destined to do it. "I'm not sure how much a choice you make to do this job. For me it's in my DNA. I was born to do this work. I couldn't image not being in service, in public service in some way."

CONTRIBUTORS

TODD BRADLEY is an associate professor of political science at Indiana University Kokomo. His research areas include civil society actors like non-profits and nongovernmental organizations and the roles they play in democratization efforts in developing countries. His other areas of research focus on the impact of ethnicity/religion on immigration issues.

ADAM R. SMITH is an assistant professor of management at Indiana University Kokomo. He earned a Ph.D. in Business Administration from the University of Tennessee, where he studied organizations and strategy and industrial-organizational psychology, and conducted research in the areas of innovation and entrepreneurship. Smith has worked in leadership development for executive MBA programs, and he has assessed more than one hundred candidates as a consultant for assessment centers that evaluate job candidates' managerial potential.

ANDREAS SCHMID is an assistant professor of health management at the University of Bayreuth, Germany. He studied Health Management and Economics at the University of Bayreuth and was a visiting scholar at the Department of Health Policy and Management at the University of North Carolina at Chapel Hill. His research focus is on hospital markets and on the coordination and collaboration of health care providers. Schmid also engages in comparative work focusing on the United States and Germany.

INDEX

A

Affordable Care Act. *See* Patient
Protection and Affordable Care
Act (2010)
African Americans: demographic
changes, 7, 8; equal oppor-
tunities, 12; nonprofit sector
workforce, 44
American healthcare system.
See health-care management
Annie E. Casey Foundation, 44, 45
anti-governmental political groups,
9, 14–15, 16, 19
Asian population: demographic
changes, 7, 8, 44; nonprofit
sector workforce, 44
Aviv, Diana, 27–28, 30

B

Battlecreek, Michigan, 45
best practices philosophy, 22,
48, 54
"big" government, 10
Bismarck, Otto von, 35
boards of directors: development
and training, 48–49; members
as potential candidates, 47–48;
nonprofit succession planning,
26, 27–28, 43, 49, 54, 55,
58–59, 61–62, 64; political
balance, 61
Board Source, 48
Brown, Willie, 11, 12, 15–16,
18, 21
budget constraints, 21, 22, 59,
60, 62
business sector, 4

C

Carpenter, Ron, 45, 48, 49
Casey Foundation, 44, 45
Center for Effective Philanthropy,
48
Center on Community
Philanthropy, ix–x, 43, 51
church-based nonprofit hospitals,
38
Clinton School of Public Service,
ix, x, xi, 43, 51
coalitions, 15, 16–17, 20
Coleman, Michael, 11, 12, 13, 15
collaborative leadership, 11, 15,
16–17, 20
community philanthropy, ix–x
conflict government, 14
contentious legislation, 19

D

David and Lucile Packard
Foundation, 44, 47
DAX Performance Index, 38
Dean, Lloyd, 11, 12, 15, 20–21, 22
demographic changes, 7, 31, 34,
36, 44
Denmark, 36
Dignity Health, 20–21, 22
diversity: Dignity Health, 20–21,
22; executive leadership, 8, 31,
44, 49; nonprofit sector workforce, 44; nonprofit succession
planning, 26, 30–31; recruitment efforts, 49

E

early retirement practices, 36
economic crises, 36
economic dynamics, 4–5
Eugene and Agnes E. Meyer
Foundation, 46
Evelyn and Walter Hass Jr.
Fund, 44
executive leadership: boards of
directors, 27–28, 43; demographic changes, 8; diversity, 8,
31, 44, 49; functional role, 5–6;
management competencies,
28–29, 39–40; motivational
sources and styles, 10, 11–14,
22–24; succession manage-
ment, 26–27, 37–41, 44–45;
training opportunities, 37–38,
41; turnover rates, 38; value
systems, 22–23, 29–30, 39
external recruitment, 38–39, 49,
55, 57–59
extrinsic motivation, 10, 22

F

female executives, 44
Ferrari, Pierre, 27, 29, 30, 31
financial crises, 36
fiscal dynamics, 4–5
Ford Foundation, 47
for-profit healthcare systems, 29,
34, 38, 39, 41, 60, 62–64
foundations: internal talent, 46–48;
research methodology, 45;
succession management and
planning, 43–46
Frankfort, Indiana, 16
French Revolution, 3
fundraising responsibilities, 61

G

gender diversity, 44

generational transformations,
19–20
generation Y, 9, 17–18
German healthcare system, 33–41
givers, 10
government sector, 4–5
greater good philosophy, 30
Greater Kansas City Community
Foundation, 45–46
Greenleaf, Robert, 18
gross domestic product (GDP),
4, 5

H

Hacker, Jan, 34, 35, 37, 39
Hamilton, Lee, 9, 11, 12, 14,
15, 17, 21, 22
health-care management:
American-German com-
monalities, 33–41; budget
constraints, 59, 62; challenges, 64–65; leadership
competencies, 39–40; mergers
and acquisitions, 41, 62–64;
next-generation nonprofit leaders, 39–40, 41; nursing positions, 57; small rural hospitals,
56–63; succession management
and planning, 53–65
Health Insurance Act (1883), 35
Heifer International, 27, 29, 30
Horn, Jerome, 56–65
hospital turnover rates, 38, 59.
See also health-care
management

I

ideological challenges, 19
immigrant populations, 7–8
Independent Sector, 27, 44
Indiana State University
Foundation, 45, 47–48
individual leadership capital, 20

internal talent, 31–32, 46–48, 57–58, 59–60
international comparisons, 33–41
internship opportunities, 30
intrinsic motivation, 10, 11–14, 22–23

J

Johnson, Kevin, 11, 12, 13–14, 18, 23

K

Kaiser Permanente, 20, 27
Kansas City, Missouri, 46
Kellogg Foundation, 45, 47
Kennedy, John F., 9

L

Larson, Carol, 47
Latino population: demographic changes, 7, 8, 44; nonprofit sector workforce, 44
leadership challenges: capital resources, 20; foundations, 46; future outlook, 24; local government, 10–11; minority populations, 44; negative perceptions, 14–17; obstacles, 19–21; value systems, 22–23, 29–30, 39. *See also* Motivating Crowding Theory; succession management and planning
leadership competencies: executive leadership, 28–29; foundations, 46–48; health-care management, 39–40
leadership from within. *See* internal talent
Little Rock, Arkansas, 45
local government challenges, 10–11

M

managerial leadership capital, 20
mandatory health insurance, 35
Marshall, Thurgood, 13
matchers, 10
McBarnes, Chris, 9, 11, 12, 16, 18
mergers and acquisitions, 41, 62–64
Meyer Foundation, 46
Mineola, Texas, 12
minority populations: demographic changes, 7, 8, 44; nonprofit sector workforce, 44
Motivating Crowding Theory: basic concepts, 9–10; collaborative partnerships, 11, 15, 16–17, 20; extrinsic motivation, 10, 22; generational transformations, 19–20; generation Y, 17–18; importance, 22–23; influencing factors, 23–24; intrinsic motivation, 10, 11–14, 22–23. *See also* leadership challenges

N

networks, 16–17
Neumann, Jens-Peter, 34, 35, 38
next-generation nonprofit leaders, 25–32, 39–40, 41, 50–51
nonprofit sector, 4–8, 44
nonprofit succession planning: basic concepts, 26–27; board development and training, 48–49; as board of directors responsibility, 26, 27–28, 43, 49, 54, 55, 58–59, 61–62, 64; budget constraints, 59, 60, 62; challenges, 25–26, 64–65; criticisms, 6; demographic changes, 7–8; diversity issues, 26, 30–31; executive leadership, 5–6; foundations, 43–46;

German healthcare system, 37–41; health-care management, 53–65; importance, 53–54; institutionalization, 32; internal talent, 31–32, 46–48, 57–60; international comparisons, 33–41; leadership competencies, 28–29, 39–40; mergers and acquisitions, 41, 62–64; next-generation leaders, 25–32, 39–40, 41, 50–51; nursing positions, 57; outside talent, 32, 55, 57–58; recruitment efforts, 31–32, 38–39, 49, 55, 57–59; research methodology, 26–27, 34–35, 45; retirement impacts, 37, 41, 53, 58; value-based leadership, 29–30, 39
nursing positions, 57

O

Obamacare. *See* Patient Protection and Affordable Care Act (2010)
Oklahoma City bombing, 19
origins of conflict theory, 14
other-oriented motivation, 10
outside talent, 32, 55, 57–58

P

Packard Foundation, 44, 47
partnerships, 15, 16–17, 20
Patient Protection and Affordable Care Act (2010), 34
philanthropic organizations. *See* foundations
policymaking comparisons, 35
political leadership capital, 20
private-sector: health-care management, 54; motivational factors, 22, 24; succession management and planning, 55
public-service sector: collaborative partnerships, 11, 15, 16–17,

20; executive leadership, 5–6, 22–24, 51; future outlook, 24; historical perspective, 3–4; leadership challenges, 10–11, 14–15, 19–24; motivational sources and styles, 10, 11–14, 22–24; negative perceptions, 14–17; research methodology, 9, 11; succession management and planning, 38, 54, 60, 62, 64–65; turnover rates, 15, 38, 59. *See also* next-generation nonprofit leaders

R

reciprocity, 10
recruitment efforts, 31–32, 38–39, 49, 55, 56, 57–59
retirement impacts, 36, 37, 41, 46, 50, 53, 58
Rüter, Georg, 34–35, 37, 39, 40

S

San Francisco Foundation, 44
San Francisco State University, 12
self-governing traditions, 4
servant leadership movement, 18
small rural hospitals, 56–63
social media, 16
spatial assimilation, 7
Speirn, Sterling, 45, 47, 48–49, 50
Spelman College, 20, 22
"stand your ground" laws, 19
Stark, Donna, 45
succession management and planning: basic concepts, 26–27; board development and training, 48–49; as board of directors responsibility, 26, 27–28, 43, 49, 54, 55, 58–59, 61–62, 64; budget constraints, 59, 60, 62; challenges, 25–26, 64–65; criticisms, 6; demographic changes, 7–8; diversity

issues, 26, 30–31; executive leadership, 5–6; federal government, 21; foundations, 43–46; German healthcare system, 37–41; health-care management, 53–65; importance, 53–54; institutionalization, 32; internal talent, 31–32, 46–48, 57–60; international comparisons, 33–41; leadership competencies, 28–29, 39–40; mergers and acquisitions, 41, 62–64; next-generation leaders, 25–32, 39–40, 41, 50–51; nursing positions, 57; outside talent, 32, 55, 57–58; recruitment efforts, 31–32, 38–39, 49, 55, 57–59; research methodology, 26–27, 34–35, 45; retirement impacts, 37, 41, 53, 58; value-based leadership, 29–30

T

Tabron, LaJune Montgomery, 47
takers, 10
Tea Party, 9, 14, 15, 16, 19, 23–24
Terre Haute, Indiana, 45
terrorist attacks, 19
third-party government system, 4, 5

Tocqueville, Alexis de, 3
Twain, Mark, 10
Tyson, Barnard, 27, 28–29

U

United States healthcare system. *See* health-care management
Upjohn Pharmaceutical Company, 12

V

value-based leadership, 22–23, 29–30, 39
volunteerism, 3, 19, 30

W

Walker, Darren, 47
West, Sherece, 45, 47, 48, 50–51
White, Leonard, 19
"wicked problems," 15
Willie Brown Institute, 21
Wilson, James Q., 35
Winthrop Rockefeller Foundation, 45, 47
W. K. Kellogg Foundation, 45, 47

DR. KARL BESEL has served as the assistant dean and director of the School of Public and Environmental Affairs at Indiana University Northwest since July of 2015. Prior to that he was the graduate program director and professor of public administration and health management at Indiana University Kokomo. Dr. Besel has also worked as a research professor and center director at the University of Louisville, as well as being an executive director of a court-related nonprofit organization. In 2014 he was named a Distinguished William J. Clinton Lecturer. Dr. Besel also served as the Visiting Scholar of Community Philanthropy at the Center on Community Philanthropy, Clinton School of Public Service (University of Arkansas) in 2009. He holds a doctoral degree from the School of Business from the University of Louisville, Kentucky, where he specialized in organizational administration, and he also received a graduate degree in social work (MSSW) from the University of Louisville, and a bachelor's degree from Valparaiso University.

CHARLOTTE LEWELLEN WILLIAMS, DRPH, MPH, is associate professor of public health and director of the Center on Community Philanthropy (The Center) at the University of Arkansas Clinton School of Public Service. She holds an adjunct faculty appointment in the University of Arkansas for Medical Sciences (UAMS) Office of Global Health and is associate faculty with the University of Arkansas at Little Rock Institute on Race and Ethnicity. Williams serves on the University of Arkansas at Little Rock Chancellor's Committee on Race and Ethnicity. A business administration graduate from Howard University, Washington, DC, Williams earned her doctoral and master's degrees in public health from the UAMS College of Public Health. In her academic research experience, she has extensively studied and published papers in several peer-reviewed journals including *Academic Medicine,* the *Journal of Communication,* and *the Journal of Nonprofit Management and Leadership*